C000242107

BLOOD, SWEAT AND TYRES

THE LITTLE BOOK OF THE AUTOMOBILE

DAVID LONG

WITH ILLUSTRATIONS BY LES EVANS

The History Press

'The more I drive in this semi-autonomous country of
asphalt, the more the behaviour of its citizens just seems
rich, baffling and strange.'

Joe Moran, On Roads

Ego autem coacervavi omne quod inveni

First published 2010

The History Press
The Mill, Brimscombe Port
Stroud, Gloucestershire, GL5 2QG
www.thehistorypress.co.uk

© David Long, 2010

The right of David Long to be identified as the Author
of this work has been asserted in accordance with the
Copyrights, Designs and Patents Act 1988.

All rights reserved. No part of this book may be reprinted
or reproduced or utilised in any form or by any electronic,
mechanical or other means, now known or hereafter invented,
including photocopying and recording, or in any information
storage or retrieval system, without the permission in writing
from the Publishers.

British Library Cataloguing in Publication Data.
A catalogue record for this book is available from the British Library.

ISBN 978 0 7524 5488 7
Typesetting and origination by The History Press
Printed in Great Britain

CONTENTS

MOTORING'S SEVEN DEADLY SINS

Lust
In a survey carried out by *Men's Journal* 86 per cent of readers said they would sooner drive the latest Range Rover than date Claudia Schiffer.

Pride
London's first traffic island was installed in St James's Street off Piccadilly in order that its inventor could cross safely to his club. Unfortunately, glancing round to admire it, Colonel Pierpoint was knocked down by a cab.

Gluttony
Autocar magazine once calculated that transporting overweight motorists in the US cost a billion extra gallons of petrol a year.

Wrath
Furious that his new De Tomaso Pantera sports car wouldn't start one morning, Elvis Presley pulled out a handgun and shot it.

Envy
Jealously guarding its reputation in the 1950s, Rolls-Royce refused to sell its Phantom IV to anyone except Britain's royal family and other heads of state.

Avarice
Saudi King Ibn Saud had a solid silver washbasin in his limo and a semi-circular seat so he could sit in the back cross-legged.

Sloth
The first Englishwoman ever to be fined for speeding, the Hon. Mrs Victor Bruce, protested to the court that, 'driving slowly makes me tired.' She should have bought a Renault 16, the first car in which the front and rear seats folded down to make a double bed.

MOTORIOUS CARBARIANS: THE EARLY DAYS

A hundred years ago you could drive all day without seeing another car, indeed passing motorists were so rare they would cheerily wave hullo. AA patrolmen were similarly required in the early days to give respectful salutes to their motorised masters, and the dictionary's only definition of 'jam' referred to something you spread on your toast at breakfast.

Sounds good, but in some quarters the motorist was already morphing into Public Enemy No. 1, *The Times* railing against what it called 'motorious carbarians' and others in authority seriously suggesting that these new-fangled automobiles be fitted with explosive devices set to automatically detonate if its goggle-wearing driver went over a certain (very modest) speed. In London the Marquess of Queensbury even went to court to obtain legal permission to shoot dead any motorist whom he considered a danger to him or his family.

The police weren't too happy about their activities scaring the horses either, and its officers – for many years denied vehicles of their own (until 1920, happy days) – were at one point issued with so-called 'egg-bombs', a kind of explosive paint-filled grenade, for hurling at misbehaving motorists. The motorcar's progress, however, was to be unstoppable, as the following, highly selective, timeline suggests.

1770: Nicolas-Joseph Cugnot completes his *Voiture en Petit*, the first road-going machine to move under artificial power (in this case steam) managing 2.5mph for 15 minutes before its boiler needed refuelling.

1824: In South London Samuel Brown's 4hp 'gas-vacuum engine' successfully climbs Shooter's Hill, but it costs so much more to run than the rival steam engine that the idea is not pursued.

1832: The first of an incredible 30 million motorised fatalities occurs – so far, that is – when *The Enterprise*, a steam omnibus, explodes killing a stoker travelling between the City and Paddington.

1893: For 25*s* a week Frederick Simms rents a workshop beneath a railway arch in Putney, South London, since identified by an official English Heritage blue plaque as 'the birthplace of the motor industry in Britain'.

1895: The Hon. Evelyn Ellis MP becomes one of the first to drive a car in Britain, technically an illegal act at a time when the law requires self-propelled vehicles to be preceded by a walking man carrying a red flag.

1896: In London his pal Lord Winchilsea, chairman of the Great Horseless Carriage Company, ceremoniously tears up the hated red flag to celebrate the speed limit being raised from 4mph to a heady 12mph.

1900: Terms such as 'garage' and 'motorist' enter the English lexicon for the first time, but most drivers – typically at this time hippophilic aristocrats – continue to refer to their mechanics as 'motor grooms'.

1901: Within a year Britain boasts an estimated 8,000 motor vehicles, approximately one per 4,750 head of population. By the end of the decade the ratio is closer to 1:770.

1905: Coventry boasts no fewer than 29 indigenous motor manufacturers, but of London's 10,380 licensed taxicabs only 19 are motorised with the vast majority still horse-drawn.

1909: Across the Atlantic, and against a tide of new marques and models, Senator Joseph W. Bailey of Texas continues to insist that, 'if I had my way I would make it a crime to use automobiles on the public highway.'

1910: Britain's first ever sports car goes on sale – the truly splendid Vauxhall Prince Henry – but is inexplicably named after a Prussian nobleman.

1911: A Model T Ford becomes the first car ever to scale Ben Nevis and the inaugural Monte Carlo Rally takes place – making it motorsport's oldest surviving fixture. It is closely followed by the first ever Indianapolis 500 which was won by Ray Harroun who equips his Marmon 'Wasp' with a new invention called a rear-view mirror.

1912: Aptly named, the Peugeot Bébé goes on sale in France and is so small that the passenger has to sit slightly aft of the driver to give him sufficient elbow-room to steer.

1913: Travelling by ship the engine pioneer Rudolf Christian Karl Diesel falls overboard and is drowned.

1914: Desperate to move men to the Western Front as quickly as possible, France's General Gallieni requisitions 600 Renault taxis offering their owner-drivers a 27 per cent tip on top of the meter price to ferry troops to Nanteuil.

1915: Recognising an unstoppable trend, Edinburgh's Caledonian Hotel offers guests a special chauffeur's rate of only 7s 6d (37.5p) for bed, breakfast, lunch and dinner.

1916: Eleanor Thornton, the model for Rolls-Royce's famous 'Spirit of Ecstasy' radiator mascot, is lost at sea when the ship on which she is travelling to Egypt is torpedoed by the German Navy.

1917: Somewhat belatedly, Japan joins the motor industry with the launch of the country's first series production car, the Mitsubishi Model-A.

1918: American motor industry pioneer Walter P. Chrysler buys his first car, learns how to drive it on the way home, and then when he gets there dismantles it to discover how it all works.

1919: Britain's first roadside petrol pump is installed at Hale, Manchester. It's not far from Ford's first overseas factory and within a year an incredible 40 per cent of all the cars on Britain's roads are Model T Fords.

1921: Warren G. Harding becomes the first US president to travel to his inauguration by motorcar: a 1920 Packard Twin Six.

1926: Britain's Sir Henry Segrave sets a new world record for the flying kilometre, his Sunbeam Tiger actually leaving the ground and one point and 'flying' nearly 50ft.

1929: The car used in the Valentine's Day Massacre is another Packard, cunningly disguised to look like a Lincoln squad car.

NOTABLE BRITISH MOTORING FIRSTS

First Traffic Island
This handy refuge for pedestrians, strategically placed midstream between two lines of traffic, was invented by a doubtless whiskery Victorian, Colonel Pierpoint, who in 1864 positioned his prototype so that he could cross the road safely to get to his club in St James's. Unfortunately the colonel was in the habit of turning round to admire his creation each time he used it, and on one such occasion missed his footing and was promptly hit by a cab.

First Mechanical Cab
In those days of course his nemesis would have arrived with a horse up front, as the first mechanically driven hackney cabs didn't make an appearance until 1897. These early ones were battery-powered, which made them nice and clean and quiet, but also so heavy that they were markedly slower than the horses they were meant to replace.

First Parking Meter
The parking meter was invented in America – Archie Arnold of Harlan, Indiana, so hated them that when he died he had two erected on his grave, both indicating 'Time Expired' – but the first to come to Britain in 1958 was put up in Mayfair, London, at a time when one shilling (5p) would buy you a full hour. Today the same sum is good for less than a minute.

First Drive-In Bank
Britain's first drive-in bank was in London too, Drummonds just off Trafalgar Square, but its first set of traffic lights – being gas-powered – was less of a success and blew up in 1868, killing a policeman and causing a passing platoon of cavalry to stampede. The first self-service petrol station flopped badly too, the shilling-in-a-slot meters at Patcham in East Sussex in the 1930s proving far too simple for passing motorists to fiddle.

First Motorway

Lord Montagu of Beaulieu supported the idea of a high-speed carriageway linking London and Liverpool back in 1924 – the same year the Italians built the world's first motorway or *autostrada* – but it took more than three decades before anything was done about it. The first opened in 1958 as the Preston Bypass – today it is part of the M6 – and motorists were warned not to picnic on the verges and that anyone caught driving the wrong way along it would be fined £20.

First Belisha Beacon

As well as introducing the eponymous beacon while Minister for Transport, Leslie Hore-Belisha MP (1893–1957) was responsible for a number of innovations including the 30mph limit and the driving test. However he lost his seat in the Cabinet, not because these were unpopular but because an orchestrated campaign of anti-Semitic mumblings followed the announcement that he, a Jew, was to become the next Secretary of State for War.

First Speeding Ticket

Britain's first ever speeding ticket was handed out by Hampshire Constabulary. In 1895 they fined John Koosen a shilling for driving at a reckless 6mph, with an additional 15s 7d legal costs making a grand total of nearly 83p for a first offence.

First Motor Show

The world's first ever motor show was held in Tunbridge Wells, Kent, the brainchild of Sir David Salomans who undertook to exhibit his 'Petroleum Carriage' – an early Peugeot – at 3 p.m. on 15 October 1895 on the town's Agricultural Show Ground. More than 5,000 spectators turned up to see it, together with the Count de Dion's steam tractor, a 'one mouse-power' tricycle, and a petrol-driven fire engine provided by Frederick Simms.

First Garage

A keen pipe-smoker and philanthropist, Sir David was also among the first to fit out his house with a well-equipped 'motor house' although the one he built on his Broomhill estate was a poor relation of Sir Edward Nichol's. This was fitted out with panelling removed from Edward VII's robing room at the Palace of Westminster in order to provide suitably grand surroundings for Sir Edward's pair of Rolls-Royces.

First Multi-Storey Car Park

The country's first ever multi-storey car park was constructed just off Piccadilly Circus in central London. This was back in May 1901, when cars were still a real rarity, and was located in Denman Street (where today NCP offers a similar service). The world's largest car park at the time, it covered more than 19,000sq ft, and with seven storeys the upper levels were reached via a hydraulic lift which was capable of raising a 3-ton vehicle.

First Electric Self-Starter

Cadillac in 1912 may have become the first company to fit electric starting kits to its cars as standard, but as early as 1896 an Englishman – known only as Mr Dowsing – fitted a self-starter to his Kent-built Arnold-Benz 1.5-litre. A more convenient, all-weather 'indoor' starting handle was also a British innovation, introduced on the Trojan as early as 1922.

First Purpose-Built Race Track

With racing on the public highway outlawed in Britain – hence the Tourist Trophy taking place offshore, on the Isle of Man – a poodle-breeding jigsaw-puzzle addict called Hugh Fortescue Locke-King hatched a plan to build a proper circuit on his estate south of London. To this end some 2,000 Surrey labourers removed 30 acres of woodland and half a million tons of mud to make way for the historic Brooklands banked track near Weybridge.

First Front-Wheel Drive Grand Prix Car

In 1926 Alvis produced a front-wheel drive car, just in time to miss that year's British Grand Prix. In fact this probably didn't matter, rear-wheel drive being so obviously superior that, despite attempts continuing into the mid-1950s, no front-wheel drive car has ever won a GP.

First Gas Turbine Car in F1

Originally built to compete in the Indianapolis 500, the Lotus 56B with its Pratt & Whitney turbine – and what the race commentator called 'the biggest brake pedal ever seen in F1' – was modified in time for the 1971 Brands Hatch Race of Champions but retired when its suspension failed. Driver Emerson Fittipaldi took it out again at Silverstone, coming third, but the technology turned out to be another blind alley.

First Person to Drive to Australia

Piloting a modestly powered 14hp Bean, Mr Francis Birtles motored overland from London to Sydney, setting off on 19 October 1927 and arriving on 15 July the following year.

First Car Air Ferry

In October 1946 a car was airlifted from Reading to Guernsey for a Channel Island car dealer, but the first regular service started three years later when Silver City Airways inaugurated the world's first car air ferry service from Port Lympne in Kent to Le Touquet using comically bulbous Bristol Freighters.

First Swivelling Headlights

Now making a bit of a comeback, Citroën is generally credited with the invention of lamps which turn with the wheels in 1967 although Earl Mountbatten of Burma always insisted he had fitted them to his own car at least a decade earlier and claimed also to have invented dipped headlamps.

First Sliding Doors

Though only a one-off, a convertible Bentley by coachbuilder James Young of Bromley appeared at the 1935 London Motor Show pre-empting the likes of the Peugeot 1007 and Fiat Ulysse by more than half a century. We can claim electric window lifts too, Daimler having introduced these as an option on its 1946 DE36, while Triumph was first with screen washers as standard, in 1935.

BRITAIN'S MOTORWAY MADNESS

Announcing their grand scheme for a network of new motorways crisscrossing the country in the 1950s, Ministry of Transport planners sketched out the first 1,000 miles in coloured crayon on a map given away free with a copy of *Tit-Bits* magazine.

When work started it was on a similarly make-do-and-mend basis. Among the bulldozers used to build the M6, for example, were several redundant Second World War Sherman tanks while the concrete runway at Heston Aerodrome – where Mr Chamberlain waved his useless piece of paper – was hastily redeployed as part of the M4.

Amazingly when it came to clearing a path for the M1, contractors had to demolish just five houses and a trio of bungalows near Luton. However, so many Irish navvies were needed to remove 14,000,000 cubic yards of topsoil that two Catholic priests were imported from Kerry and Armagh to hear confessions in huts provided for this purpose.

The first traffic cone resulted from a failed attempt to mould the trunk of a plastic toy elephant.

The M4 was the first British motorway to be designed by computer, the M6 Toll Road consumed 2.5 million pulped Mills and Boon novels in its construction, and the M5 is known to be used by thousands of migrating birds as an aid to navigation.

Spaghetti Junction near Birmingham covers 30 acres, weighs 250,000 tons and required the rescue of a quarter of a million fish living in a pond which the roadbuilders needed to fill-in. Bizarrely the stanchions beneath the roadway were designed in such a way that a horse-drawn barge could in theory still use the canal down below.

Despite appearances the M25 is not a complete ring road as it briefly becomes the A282 while crossing the Thames at Dartford. Bob Geldof worked for a while on one of its construction crews before achieving greater fame as a Boomtown Rat and today what may turn out to be his most enduring creation is lit by 10,606 lights and 2,959 illuminated road signs.

The first person to be arrested for flying under a motorway bridge was stunt pilot Joan Hughes who doubled for Lady Penelope in a live-action scene from a 1968 *Thunderbirds* movie which was shot on the M40 near High Wycombe.

When Jimi Hendrix first arrived in the country he heard so many gigging musicians talking about the Blue Boar that he thought it was a concert venue rather than a service station on the M1.

Despite the fact that we think our roadsigns are better than anyone else's – and where do you think 1970s prog-rockers Hatfield and the North got the name from? – the familiar sans-serif typeface used on British motorways is based on an 1890s German font with the rather unattractive name, *Akzidenx Grotesk*.

AND SPEAKING OF ABROAD: WHERE LEFT IS RIGHT…

Back in the day when travellers passing each other on foot or horseback might have needed to protect themselves, logic suggested that (most of us being right handed) one ought to keep to the left as that way it is easier to draw a sword.

The practice of doing it this way was formalised in a Papal Edict to pilgrims by Pope Boniface in about 1300, and certainly we Brits like to think he got it right. The reality however is that most of the world does it the other way round and persists in driving on the wrong side of the road. Sweden used to be with us – it swapped from one side of the street to the other over the course of a weekend in 1967 – but these days with only a few exceptions (Japan, most notably) it is as a rule only former and existing British colonies which still drive on the left.

Anguilla	Dominica	Kiribati
Antigua and Barbuda	East Timor	Lesotho
Australia	Falkland Islands	Macau
Bahamas	Fiji	Malawi
Bangladesh	Grenada	Malaysia
Barbados	Guernsey	Maldives
Bermuda	Guinea	Malta
Bhutan	Guyana	Mauritius
Botswana	Hong Kong	Montserrat
Brunei	India	Mozambique
Cayman Islands	Indonesia	Namibia
Central African	Ireland	Nauru
Republic	Isle of Man	Nepal
Christmas Island	Jamaica	New Zealand
Cocos Islands	Japan	Niue
Cook Islands	Jersey	Norfolk Island
Cyprus	Kenya	Pakistan

Papua New Guinea	Singapore	Trinidad and Tobago
Pitcairn Islands	Solomon Islands	Turks and Caicos
St Helena	South Africa	Islands
St Kitts and Nevis	Sri Lanka	Tuvalu
St Lucia	Suriname	Uganda
St Vincent and the	Swaziland	United Kingdom
Grenadines	Tanzania	Virgin Islands
Salvador	Thailand	Zambia
Samoa	Tokelau	Zimbabwe
Seychelles	Tonga	

... AND WHERE IT'S NOT

By contrast the following countries have actually banned right-hand-drive cars, although in some cases – such as the first named, where such cars are illegally imported from neighbouring Thailand – they are by no means uncommon.

Cambodia
Gambia
Ghana
Oman
Philippines
Slovakia
Taiwan

Closer to home another peculiarity is Savoy Court, running off the Strand in central London and the only street in the UK where vehicles are required to drive on the right. The origin of this is obscure, although one possible reason could date from the early days of the black cab when the driver would reach behind him to open the passenger door (which opened backwards and had the handle at the front) so that his fare could enter the hotel.

The practice of invaders forcing residents to switch from one side to the other is also encountered occasionally. There is no evidence that this practice was introduced by Napoleon because he so hated the English, but the Nazis certainly required such a change to be made in Austria, Czechoslovakia, Hungary and the Channel Islands. The Argentinians did likewise during their brief tenure of the Falkland Islands, and East Timor changed to driving on the left under Indonesian rule in the mid-1970s.

Okinawa similarly changed, but from left to right, from 1945 to 1972 while it was under US control.

Finally one cannot help but notice that many of the smartest marques were for a long time with us on this one. Despite building Rolls-Royces in America for many years, the company stuck with right-hand drive until 1923. Pierce Arrow completely refused to build left-hookers, maintaining that right-hand-drive was more convenient for owners' chauffeurs. Neither would Ettore Bugatti ever authorise a car to be built with his name on it and the steering wheel on the wrong side, while Lancia only made the switch in 1956 and then only because it was keen to sell more cars to Americans.

WISH YOU WEREN'T HERE: 10 PLACES WORTH AVOIDING FOR A DRIVING HOLIDAY

Egypt: where someone is killed or seriously injured every 30 minutes.

Ethiopia: where the death rate is exactly 100 times worse than in overcrowded Japan.

Greece: where the picture's so bad that for years the government actually refused to publish any road accident statistics.

India: where car ownership is spiralling rapidly, the driving test's so simple it's a joke, and 600 die every month just in Delhi.

Kenya: where the death rate on the road is 10 times worse than even the worst place in Europe (and 40 times worse than in Britain).

Mexico: where one major bus operator runs under the banner 'Better Dead than Late'. If only they were joking. . . .

Pakistan: where a combination of fast trucks driving two abreast and slow-paced ox-carts meet with deadly consequences.

Portugal: where speed is considered a cheap aphrodisiac and the average fine costs less than a meal for two.

South Africa: where up to 30 deaths a day means there's nothing funny about those comically overcrowded minibuses.

THESE FUELISH THINGS:
THE POWER TO MOVE YOU

Early Alternatives

In 1911 Isaac Smyth successfully patented a car fuelled by gravity although there is no evidence that he ever managed to build one or to get it to work.

TNT, dynamite, nitro-glycerine and petrol were just four of the ingredients in a failed 1931 land speed record bid.

Rudolf Diesel's original engine was designed to run on coal-dust, with many other substances being tried – including naphtha, coal-gas, wood and wood alcohol – before oil-derived fuels began their unstoppable ascendancy.

In the early days no fewer than 180 different makes of steam-powered car were registered, mostly but not entirely in the US, and for a long time it looked as though steam rather than petrol or diesel would become the default option for the average motorist.

Theodore Roosevelt routinely used a White steamer for official functions, and – perhaps encouraged by this presidential seal of approval – in 1908 the NYPD bought several of their own to use as squad cars (known as 'prowlers').

Some of the early steam cars were also formidable racers, occasionally outlawed because it was hard to fairly assess their horsepower ratings, but managing to take the land speed record on two occasions (see p. 75) and to win a number of major races including the prestigious 1903 Paris–Madrid.

Besides White, another of the more popular makes was the Stanley, the Stanley brothers selling their company for a heady quarter of a million bucks (in 1899) and later buying it back again for just $20,000. Production at their factory peaked at 650 cars a year in 1912 – but then barely a decade later Henry Ford was producing more Model Ts than this in a single day.

In the end the steamer was probably killed off by economics as much as anything else: the superb Doble-Detroit Model F was refined and capable of 95mph in 1930 but it cost more than twice as much as the equivalent Rolls-Royce....

Electricity Sparks Enthusiasm

Between 1896 and 1939 an incredible 565 different makes of car were registered using electric power, many providing an apparently viable alternative to their established petrol- and steam-powered rivals, although the majority were built in only tiny numbers.

For example, and as previously noted, the first motorised taxis were battery powered – 77 of them being operated by the London Electric Cab Company before it was declared bankrupt in 1900. Ironically, given the Americans' marked reluctance in recent years to embrace anything but gasoline technology, the battery cabs fared rather better in New York at this time – especially the wonderfully named Morris & Salom Electrobat.

Then, as now, part of the problem was caused by the limitations of battery technology, although for a while it looked as though the great Thomas A. Edison would ride to the rescue. With some 1,093 US patents to his name, America's most prolific inventor claimed his 'wonder battery' would solve the problem of both weight and range but in the end nothing of the sort ever materialised.

Nevertheless the first car to reach a landmark 100kph was an electric one, Camille Jenatzy's wonderful *La Jamais Contente* hitting 65.7mph in April 1899 to claim the world land speed record. The American Charles Baker hoped to beat him three years later, and indeed claimed to have hit 80mph before his car collapsed when he braked hard to avoid spectators running onto the course.

Queen Alexandra was also something of an electric fan, the wife of Edward VII taking delivery in 1901 of an American device called the City & Suburban Electric Phaeton which she used to drive around their Sandringham estate in Norfolk.

Finally: the Toyota Prius? Innovative? There's nothing whatever new about hybrids as the little Interurban had interchangeable petrol and electric motors back in 1905.

Petrol: That's the Spirit

In the early days petroleum was marketed not as a fuel at all but as a patent medicine, sold in small bottles as a treatment against lice and their eggs, and intended 'to remove pain and alleviate human suffering and disease.'

During the Franco-Prussian War (1870–1) the stuff was also stockpiled in the French capital for use in crude bombs against a possible German-Prussian attack. Similarly, during the rule of the Paris Commune, rumours spread about the activities of so-called *pétroleuses*, women using bottles of petrol to commit arson against city buildings.

When it finally came to be used as fuel for transport, the word 'petrol' was at first protected, having been registered as a trade name by the British wholesaler Carless, Capel & Leonard.

While these days we think of it as a single substance, petroleum actually comprises 300 different molecular compounds, mostly aliphatic hydrocarbons. It's also seasonally adjusted by the oil companies to provide satisfactory starting and driveability for different temperatures. Because of this, winter fuel is even more volatile than that which you buy in the summer.

According to the AA, getting lost costs British motorists approximately 350,000 tonnes of wasted fuel each year. (*Autocar* similarly once reported that fat motorists in the USA use an additional one billion gallons of petrol every year.)

Although on some of them you can still drive as fast as you like, it's technically illegal for a motorist to run out of fuel on a German *autobahn*.

A mere 17 per cent of the energy released by burning petrol is actually used to move a vehicle down the road. The remaining energy is emitted as heat through the exhaust and the engine's cooling and braking systems. Without this costly waste, which is to say if technology were good enough to utilise 100 per cent of the energy produced, a typical 1,400 kilogramme car travelling at 50mph would be capable of at least 185 miles to the gallon.

Obviously we're nowhere near that yet but a typical family car still manages to run approximately 40 per cent further on a gallon of petrol than its 1978 equivalent. Markedly cleaner, the same car will also take many thousands of miles to match the exhaust emissions produced by a jet ski in only 2 hours.

The extremes of performance are highly impressive too: with 5,000 horsepower, a so-called Top Fuel dragster will hit 300mph in 5 seconds, burning fuel at up to 15 gallons a mile. On the other hand, four Honda employees in Shell's Mileage Marathon once returned 8,000 mpg around the Silverstone circuit in a homemade car.

Gas Not Gasoline

During the Second World War a number of cars were successfully converted to run on gas, oil clearly being in short supply, although this meant carrying a huge bag of the stuff on your roof which made even the smartest Daimler look ridiculous. In Edinburgh a number of single-decker buses were converted in a similar fashion, their two-wheeled gas generators being towed behind and resembling up-ended oil drums.

More recently, and for not dissimilar reasons, gas has enjoyed something of resurgence. As well as saving motorists money, marked reductions in carbon monoxide, nitrogen oxide, hydrocarbons and carbon dioxide emissions are possible by switching to Compressed Natural Gas or CNG. It's true that power outputs suffer by 10 per cent or so compared to petrol – even now nothing matches petrol in terms of outright punch – but this is usually compensated for by improved throttle response and better driveability.

Liquefied Petroleum Gas (LPG) is slightly less efficient than petrol too but far cleaner and so cheaper being less heavily taxed. Unfortunately fitting a second tank to hold it takes up boot space and means you're not allowed to take your car through the Channel Tunnel. Then again, you'll be able to afford to take the ferry having saved so much filling up.

The Biofuels Fallacy

The good news about biodiesel is that you can derive the fuel from all sorts of crops, from rape to canola, palm trees to hemp. The bad news is that large-scale manufacture requires deforestation on such a scale that more CO_2 is actually created than saved. As a result Indonesia, for example, is now the third largest emitter of greenhouse gases after the hugely more industrialised USA and China.

Bioethanol is even worse, most obviously because the industrial processes required to make it take not just the land but also real food crops to turn these into fuel. Frighteningly capital intensive, very energy intensive and time consuming to produce, it's been calculated that it takes as much food to fill the tank of a Range Rover in this way as would feed a man for a year.

Finally . . .

Let's not forget chip fat. It's smelly and disgusting but it's also plentiful and potentially free. What's more it really does work if your car runs on diesel, providing you steer clear of anything containing animal fats or lard as these really do clog up the works.

BIG OIL: THE SUPERMAJORS

By 1911 John D. Rockefeller's company Standard Oil controlled 80 per cent of the US oil market, a near-monopoly which couldn't be allowed to continue, leading the government to make moves to break it into three. Together with four other major oil distributors, the resulting 'Magnificent Seven' were able to take advantage of the massive upsurge in demand to maintain a frightening level of global dominance. This in turn was only gradually reined-in as the governments of a number of foreign oil-rich states began to assert their own control over the means of production.

Standard Oil of New Jersey

The company merged with Mobil to form ExxonMobil, but is still known here as Esso, i.e. S O meaning Standard Oil. Esso originally sold its products as Pratt's Motor Car Spirit but fared rather better when advertising its smokeless paraffin. Calling it Esso Blue, the UK company produced a long-running television campaign using a witty reworking of the tune *Smoke Gets in Your Eyes*, 'They asked me how I knew/it was Esso Blue/I of course replied/with lower grades one buys/smoke gets in your eyes.'

Royal Dutch Shell

The English end of the Anglo-Dutch combine was founded by Sir Marcus Samuel, 1st Viscount Bearsted, and Samuel Samuel, whose father started in business manufacturing jewel boxes and other Victorian bric-a-brac out of seashells – hence the company's logo. Originally this featured a mussel shell before it was switched to the familiar scallop or pecten in 1904. The contract for one of the Samuels' most important oil deals was written on the back of an Orient Express menu three years later, and by 2009 the company was rated by Forbes as the world's second largest after General Electric.

Anglo-Persian Oil Company

Later renamed the Anglo-Iranian Oil Company and then British Petroleum, a merger followed with Amoco (another Standard Oil spin-off) and today the company is known by its initials BP. In 2008 it was presented with a satirical Emerald Paintbrush Award by Greenpeace, highlighting the company's skill at 'greenwashing' its activities by heavily advertising its relatively small investment in alternative energy sources while continuing to make the bulk of its investments in fossil fuel extraction.

Standard Oil Company of New York

Known as Socony, and later renamed Mobil, the company's eventual merger with Exxon marked a partial reassembly of Rockefeller's behemoth. Unusually for an oil major – particularly an American one – from 1936 to 1968 the company sponsored an economy run designed to encourage domestic auto manufacturers to see how frugally their cars could be driven across the country.

Standard Oil of California

Socal became Chevron and then, after merging with Texaco, ChevronTexaco before returning to the name Chevron. In 1933 the company was granted a concession to find oil in Saudi Arabia, and did so five years later. In the 1950s it also discovered the world's largest oil field – Ghawar, in Saudi Arabia – but in 1973 the Saudi government began buying shares in the joint venture and by 1980 was able to claim it owned the resulting entity outright.

Gulf Oil

Based for many years in Pittsburgh, until 1970 Gulf's HQ was the city's tallest building. It was further distinguished by an illuminated pyramidal summit which changed colour with changes in barometric pressure thereby providing a weather indicator which was visible from many

miles away. With the design based on the Mausoleum of Halicarnassus – one of the Seven Wonders of the Ancient World – the building is now a block of flats, Gulf itself having joined forces with Chevron in 1984 in what was at that time the largest corporate merger ever seen.

Texaco

Before merging with Chevron in 2001 'the Texas Company' had proudly claimed to be the only oil company selling petrol in all 50 states. As well as introducing standardised corporate design standards across all its filling stations back in 1937 – Art Deco was very much the favoured style – Texaco was the first to install 'rest rooms' at every station (in 1939) and two years later introduced the novelty of 24 hour opening on major highways. It did this in order that customers driving at night were never any more than a tankful away from a Texaco station.

THE COMPANY MEN

WHEN THE WHEELS COME OFF: GREAT CAR COMPANY BLUNDERS

We all make mistakes: an astrological survey in Japan has revealed that Virgos are behind the wheel in more than one-third of traffic accidents, and at the port of Dover an average of 10 cars a day conk-out because they're overloaded with cheap booze. However, such slips are nothing compared to the bad deals, hopeless miscalculations and occasionally fatally stupid mergers made by the car giants – which is worrying when you think how big and important they now are.

In fact, as the big beasts of the business world, car makers still account for about 10 per cent of global GDP, employing millions of people around the world and as many as 800,000+ workers here in the UK. That's why the big brands daren't recruit a risk-taker or entrepreneur to the top job, a Trump or a Branson. It's also why boardrooms tend to be populated by anonymous men-in-suits, cautious individuals who've been in the industry for decades, who understand the gravity of their position, and whom we like to think of as a safe pair of hands rather than mavericks, blue-sky thinkers or ideas men who fancy playing FTSE with the share price.

Well, you might like to think that, but looking at some of the decisions these types have made over the years it's hard to be sure. Being big ought to mean being smart, but sometimes it just means you just get to make even bigger, even more expensive mistakes. Consider Daimler-Benz. They don't come more established than this lot, with a heritage dating back to the very dawn of motoring when Gottlieb Daimler invented the internal combustion engine in 1883. He was raided immediately – the police thought it was a device for forging bank notes – and then shortly afterwards, having constructed the world's first petrol-powered car, Karl Benz crashed it into a brick wall.

Despite this shaky start there were still some forward thinkers, like pioneering automobilist Stanley Edge who recognised that 'this motor business will be the boom of the next century.' But at Daimler they weren't so sure, having carefully calculated that demand for these new fangled machines would never top a thousand because competent, fully trained chauffeurs would always be in short supply.

And were these guys crotchety? Oldsmobile, America's first car manufacturer, only came about because Ransom E. Olds couldn't stand the smell of horses. His rivals at Packard stuck with primitive single-cylinder engines for years, because they genuinely believed that four cylinders just meant four times as much to go wrong. Closer to home Ferry Porsche apparently hated the 928 so much that he refused to attend the award ceremony when it was named Car of the Year 1978; and as we'll see later, BMC boss Sir Leonard Lord only put the Mini into production in order to get 'these bloody awful bubble cars off the streets.'

Indeed even when cars became genuinely mass-market the bosses were so out of touch that, at the outbreak of the Second World War, General Motors boss Alfred P. Sloan declared that his company was simply 'too big to be inconvenienced by pitiful international squabbles.' Around the same time Henry Ford turned down the opportunity to build the Spitfire – as a committed anti-Semite he was betting on Hitler winning in the end – and later on his grandson missed out on the opportunity to acquire Volkswagen lock, stock and Beetle because he thought the cars the company made were completely worthless.

In fact Ford wasn't the only company to get that one wrong. Much like the Decca executive who turned down a bunch of Liverpool mop tops in the early '60s on the grounds that guitar groups were on their way out, Britain's Rootes Group went so far as to ridicule the VW Beetle publicly,

calling it ugly and 'not an example of first-rate modern design.' Younger readers probably haven't heard of Rootes, which is long defunct, but will almost certainly buy a VW at some point in their driving career. . . .

THE FIRM: KEEPING IT IN THE FAMILY

These days one tends to think of big multinationals – oil companies, carmakers – as fairly faceless corporations rather than classic mom-and-pop shops. In fact a surprising number of car companies still have founding family members on the boards, and more than a few of those families have retained a considerable measure of control.

BMW
Quandt family – 46.6 per cent.
Harald Quandt, stepson to Nazi propaganda chief Josef Goebbels, inherited a 30 per cent stake in the company when his real father, Hitler's 'Leader of the Armaments Economy', died in the 1950s.

Ferrari
Ferrari Family – 10 per cent
While the company's major shareholder is Fiat, and has been for several decades, a tenth of the shares are still controlled by Piero Lardi Ferrari, the founder's second and sole surviving son.

Fiat
Agnelli family – 30 per cent
Based in Turin, the Fabbrica Italiana Automobili Torino was founded in 1899 by a group of investors led by Giovanni Agnelli whose family still have their hands very much on the levers of power.

Ford
Ford family 40 per cent
The descendents of founder Henry Ford still own a major chunk of the voting shares in the company with Henry Ford's great-grandson, William Clay Ford Jr., the most recent to serve as chairman.

Morgan
Morgan family – 100 per cent
Worcestershire's oldest sports car manufacturer was founded by H.F.S. Morgan – after he had crashed a borrowed Benz car causing £28 worth of damage – and today is headed by his grandson Charles.

Porsche

Porsche and Piech families – 50 per cent

Two closely related families – Ferdinand Porsche's daughter married a Herr Piech – still exercise a strong hold on the fortunes of both Porsche and VW-Audi.

Peugeot-Citroën

Peugeot family – 30 per cent

Peugeot can trace its origins as a manufacturer back to the early eighteenth century with the present head of the family, Thierry Peugeot, the sixth generation to be involved in car and bicycle manufacture.

Tata

Tata family – 34 per cent

Established in 1945, the creator of the world's cheapest car and presently owner of the combined Jaguar and Land Rover brands, the Tata group is headed by Ratan N. Tata of the founding family.

HELLO BOYS: SMOOTH WORDS FROM THE HIDDEN PERSUADERS

When it comes to what the Americans call 'selling the sizzle', few industries have invested more time and money than the carmakers. Some are so good they've almost outlived the brand, but others are so feeble you wonder how they managed to escape through the advertising agency's front door.

Audi

Vorsprung durch Technik
More horses, fewer seconds
Following your own rules
It's a miracle but we've made it

BMW

The ultimate driving machine
Man and machine in perfect harmony
Beyond logic

Buick
When better automobiles are built, Buick will build them
The Power of Understatement
You're due. Definitely due

Cadillac
You can kill a horse but not a Cadillac

Fiat
Be small again
Hand-built by robots

Honda
The Power of Dreams
Better gas mileage. A Civic responsibility

Jaguar
Grace. Pace. Space
Don't dream it, drive it

Kia
Responds to your life!

Land Rover
The Best Four by Four by Far
How the smooth take the rough

Mercedes-Benz
Engineered like no other car in the world

MG
You can do it in an MG

Nissan
Ask before you borrow it

Peugeot
More feline than ever

Renault
20km per litre, 800km per tank
Size matters

Rolls-Royce
At 60mph the loudest noise in the new Rolls-Royce comes from the electric clock

SEAT
Different rituals, same spirit

TVR
Don't just buy a car, have one made.

Toyota
Today. Tomorrow. Toyota.
Treat it with respect
Have kids. Keep your style
Mean but Green

Vauxhall
Put the fun back into driving

Volkswagen
One of the greatest pleasures you can have
For boys who were always men
Built to protect
While in Europe, pick up an ugly European
Ugly is only skin-deep

MOTORING MISFIRES:10 FALSE DAWNS

Since the actual dawn of motoring there have been plenty of false ones too: cars which sounded good or looked great but which weren't, or which simply came too late to prevent their hapless creators slipping further into the mire. Failures of the Motoring World, we salute you! (There's even a couple we wouldn't mind owning.)

1967 Toyota 2000GT
For largely snobbish reasons, no-one in Europe or the US really understood the threat from Japan until it was too late, manufacturers here tending to underestimate the appeal of good value while overestimating their own brand loyalty. Japan's early preference for building cheap and cheerful cars rather than interesting ones didn't help much either. Of course there was the odd exception, such as the Wankel-engined Mazda Cosmo (too weird for its own good), the diminutive Honda S600 with its buzzy 8,000rpm red line and a superbly taut little body, and this one, the stunning Toyota 2000GT

Favourably comparing it to Porsche's 911, *Road and Track* described it as 'one of the most enjoyable and exciting cars we've driven.' Twiggy bought one, and everyone else raved about its styling and brilliant Yamaha-tweaked double-overhead-cam straight-six. Unfortunately it cost more than the rival Porsche, and so few sold that these days most of us only know it from a white convertible's brief appearance alongside 007 in *You Only Live Twice.*

1969 Mercedes–Benz C111
The C111 saw Mercedes experimenting with a variety of new engine technologies including a direct-injection version of Felix Wankel's pioneering rotary unit. The car was visually innovative too, with gull-wing doors like the earlier 300SL, and it was fitted with a glass fibre body shell thereby sort of foreshadowing the much later carbon-bodied Mercedes-Benz McLaren SLR. Very radically styled compared to everything the company built for sale, it never made it into the showrooms although one hit 200mph at Nardo in 1978 thanks in part to an amazing drag coefficient of just 0.191. By this time the Wankel had been ditched, initially in favour of a straight-five turbo-diesel and then later a twin-turbocharged V8, although none made it into production.

1983 Alfa Romeo Arna
The name said it all, the acronym denoting *Alfa Romeo Nissan Autoveicoli* and the car itself being the result of a partnership between Italy and

Japan. The tie-up should have heralded a golden era of Euro-Asian cooperation but instead proved to be painfully short-lived. In part this was because the Arna inexplicably offered buyers the worst of both worlds – trading on each company's weaknesses by combining the styling of a late-model Nissan Cherry with technology carried over from the ageing Alfasud. Buyers would presumably have expected (and much preferred) a blend of Italian style and handling finesse combined with Japan's proven engineering know-how.

1984 Lancia Thema

Pininfarina design, a choice of luxurious, spacious saloon and estate bodies, a range of engines which included a 3.0-litre Ferrari V8, and build quality said to be equal to Fiat Group's manufacturing partner Saab's own 9000. The Thema was meant to re-establish the ailing brand as a prestige manufacturer after the mauling it received from *That's Life*, the UK tabloids and thousands of rust-afflicted Beta owners – and to be fair, with class-leading corrosion protection, the car was almost as good as they promised. Unfortunately it takes a long time to reverse a negative reputation and within a decade Lancia had given up and withdrawn from the UK to lick its wounds back at home.

1986 Rover 800

With British Leyland boss Graham Day renaming the company Rover Group in a bid to banish old associations of strike-hit Britain and poorly made products, what the company really needed was something upmarket to remind punters of quality cars like the old 3.5-litre P5 and the distinctively styled 2000 TC. They thought they'd found it in the new 800, which was closely based on the Honda Legend but embellished with extra windows, slightly crisper styling, and a more traditional 'clubby' English interior of polished wood and leather.

The range-topping Vitesse was also the fastest production Rover to date, and in the US was badged the Sterling in an attempt to foster a belief in sturdy British values. Meanwhile back at home we were treated to television advertisements mostly in German, the intention one imagines being to suggest that a positive comparison could be made with the likes of Audi and BMW. Unfortunately in the end the joke was on Rover: while the advertisement poked fun at famous buildings in Germany being designed by British architects, BMW snuck in under Honda's radar and took over Rover.

1990 Honda NSX

With its elegant aluminium architecture, handling by Ayrton Senna and that unmistakably rakish mid-engined stance, Honda's astonishing 300 horsepower NSX did a pretty good impression of contemporary Ferraris while celebrating the fact that at this time Honda was the major force in F1 having won the World Championship every single year from 1986 to 1991. Besides being much more reliable than a Ferrari, it was a good deal cheaper even though there was no skimping on such hi-tech treats as an all-aluminium monocoque and sequential multi-point fuel injection. That said it's a shame that having succeeded in creating what's been called 'the best car Ferrari never built' – although Honda preferred 'New Sportscar Experimental' or NSX – the Japanese decided not to stick with it and eventually returned to building more sensible cars like the Accord and Civic.

1998 Rover 75

Launched alongside the similarly retro Jaguar S-Type, but (aside from the hideous estate version) a more subtle and more successful reinterpretation of its parent company's design heritage, the misfortune of the 75 was to arrive on the scene too late to make a difference. Developed with help from a £700 million cash injection from BMW, and sharing some German engine and suspension components, it quickly gained a damaging reputation as an old man's car and was neither good enough to allay worries about Rover's long-term viability nor interesting enough to appeal to the kind of young buyers the ailing company badly needed to attract.

1998 New Beetle

In 1994 Volkswagen wowed US motor show visitors with a concept it called the, er, Concept 1, the creation of designer J. Mays clearly drawing its inspiration from the original Beetle. Front-engined but otherwise a good visual update, as much as anything it suggested the company did after all have a sense of humour as well as the self-confidence to look beyond all those Golf GTis and sensibly upmarket Passats. Quickly productionised it has done OK but was never as convincing as BMW's MINI or indeed Fiat's new 500.

2001 Renault Vel Satis

The latest attempt by Renault to compete with Audi, BMW and Mercedes-Benz, the company being as unable as Citroën and Peugeot to accept that no-one really believes that there's such a thing as a large, French luxury car. Together with the even more curious looking Avantime, the Vel Satis – anagrammatically unfortunately close to 'vile ★★★★' – sought

to break out of this impasse through the magic of weird styling. As a result, while Germany carried on producing a succession of sleek, svelte, elegant and well-engineered saloons, Renault pitched a curve ball with a tall, boxy shape which was way too ungainly to succeed. In a bid to lift sales off the floor the French quickly restyled a Mk II version but Renault UK wisely declined the expense of a right-hand-drive conversion.

2004 Chrysler 300C

The return of a cherished Chrysler numeric, the 300C was intended to herald the rebirth of the third of America's 'Big Three' by combining chromey US looks with proven German engineering. With elements of both Bentley and the Green Hornet's 'Black Beauty', the car's styling, like Marmite, quickly polarised opinion. Fitted with a 6.1-litre Hemi V8 the SRT version certainly shifted, but European sales limped along relying mostly on a rather more economical 3.0-litre diesel borrowed from a previous-generation Mercedes-Benz.

MOTORING MENAGERIE:
BEASTS ON CAR BADGES (PAST AND PRESENT)

Beetle   Voisin (France) Scarab (USA)

Bull   Lamborghini (Italy)

Deer/Stag	Perodua (Malaysia), Triumph (UK), Volga (Russia), Buick (US)
Dog	Sunbeam-Talbot (UK), DFP (UK)
Eagle/Hawk	Chenard-Walcker (France), Duesenburg (USA), Bianchi (Italy), Buick (USA)
Griffin	Vauxhall (UK), Saab (Sweden)
Horse	Ferrari (Italy), Porsche (Germany), Ford (US), Maya GT (UK)
Jaguar	Jaguar (UK)
Lion	Peugeot (France), Holden (Australia), Bean (UK), Argyll (UK)
Martlet	Cadillac (USA)
Ox	Morris (UK)
Ram	Dodge (USA)
Scorpion	Abarth (Italy)
Snake	Alfa Romeo (Italy), Shelby (USA)
Swallow	Simca (France)
Swift	Swift (UK)
Tiger	Proton (Malaysia)
Tortoise	Gordon-Keeble (UK)
Unicorn	Cadillac (USA)
Wolf	Volkwagen (Germany)
Wyvern	Vauxhall (UK)

A BASKET OF ROLLS: HOW MANY
LOTUS OWNERS DOES IT TAKE ...

Musing in the pages of Britain's *Classic and Sports Car*, magazine editor James Elliot wasn't the first to consider what might be the appropriate collective nouns for various marques and he won't be the last. A few favourites are shown below – for now we'll ignore Bristols and Willys – and the author welcomes new additions via his website (www.davidlong. info):

A bevy of Chevys
A bunch of Dafs
A chorus of Singers
A duke of Argylls
A fanny of Burneys
A gallery of Turners
A game of Checkers
A gathering of Clans
A life of Rileys
A loda Skodas
A lowering of Standards
A nest of Vipers
A series of Benz
A tea of Caddys
A tin of Beans
An eyeful of Ogles

TOP MARQUES: ESSENTIAL TRIVIA

Ferrari

We all know what 'Ferrari Red' looks like but in fact it comes in three different shades: *Rosso Corsa* – which is the one you're thinking of – metallic *Rosso Monza*, and *Rosso Scuderia*, the slightly orangey hue favoured by the Formula 1 team.

1980s TV detective Magnum only drove a Ferrari because the producers wanted a convertible and Porsche wouldn't agree to chop the top off one of its 928s.

Enzo Ferrari owned a Mini Cooper which he took out when he wanted to have fun or get out of the house. (Which might have happened quite often since his mother and wife lived in the same house even though they couldn't stand the sight of each other.)

The Lancia Stratos, Thema 8.32 and Fiat Dino all have Ferrari engines.

During its development, the Ferrari F40 averaged 187mph for more than 48 hours. A successor to the rarer and more beautiful 288 GTO – and clearly designed to compete with vehicles such as the Porsche 959 and Lamborghini Countach – it was also a timely celebration of the marque's fortieth anniversary.

Ferrari driver 'Fon' de Portago lost his pilot's licence after flying under a bridge for a $500 bet.

Ferrari's *Cavallino Rampante* emblem came from Francesco Baracca, Italy's top First World War air ace who remained unbeaten in aerial combat but was found dead – possibly after shooting himself – after unexpectedly failing to return from a mission.

In 1965 Ferraris came first, second and third at Le Mans.

Between them, Ferrari and Ford won every single F1 World Championship from 1968 through to 1983, and Alain Prost's 1990 French Grand Prix win was the Italian team's 100th grand prix victory.

John Surtees was the first Ferrari racing driver to resign his post.

The 308GT4 is the only mainstream Ferrari styled by Bertone.

Four seats and an automatic gearbox horrified the purists, but the 'family man' Ferrari 400 stayed in production longer than any other Ferrari.

Rolls-Royce
The first road test of the first ever Rolls-Royce took place on April Fool's Day 1904 but to avoid the obvious jokes the official report claimed it happened the previous day.

Designer John Blatchley always insisted he wanted his Rolls-Royce Silver Cloud to be like 'flying drawing rooms.'

Impressed by its quality, Sir Henry Royce allowed the Brough Superior to be advertised as the 'Rolls-Royce of motor cycles' but hastily withdrew his permission in 1935 when the company started building cars.

In 1942 the War Office considered scrapping all Rolls-Royce Phantom IIIs in order to use their V12 engines to launch troop-carrying gliders.

In 1946 early ram-raiders driving a Rolls-Royce stole Anne Boleyn's prayer book and Henry VIII's dagger from Hever Castle.

In the 1920s Henry Royce planned to ditch the traditional Rolls-Royce radiator but was dissuaded from doing so by his general manager.

Rolls-Royce resumed ownership of its most famous car, AX 201, the original 'Silver Ghost', after taking it in part-exchange for a 1948 Bentley MkVI. Today it's owned by rival Volkswagen.

Before co-founding the firm which bore his name, the Hon. Charles Stewart Rolls was the first person at Cambridge University to have a car – and later the first Englishman to die in an air crash.

When Rolls and Royce joined forces their first customer was Paris Singer, the sewing machine magnate's son, many of whose 22 siblings were named after the cities of their birth.

The R-Type engine which broke every world land, water and air speed record was first sketched by Sir Henry Royce using a walking stick in the sand at West Wittering.

Keen to sell his 1958 Silver Cloud, Peter Sellers placed an advertisement in *The Times* announcing 'Titled Motor Car Wishes to Dispose of Owner'.

In 1968 the registration 'RR 1' came up for sale, changing hands for more money than the Silver Shadow to which it was eventually affixed.

Ford

Ford Cortinas exported to Japan had to have their body shells slightly squeezed in order to sell within a particular tax bracket which depended on a car's overall width.

The company had its famous 'any colour you like as long as it's black' policy because no other paint dried fast enough to keep up with demand for the Model T.

The uniquely beautiful and aerodynamic Ford F3L needed only 200bhp to hit 200mph but failed to finish a single race.

The Ford Cortina is ridiculed these days but it was Britain's best-selling car for 10 years, and stayed in the top three for two whole decades.

The Ford DFV grand prix engine won its very first race and went on to score a record 155 victories between 1967 and 1983.

Ford once planned to sponsor a made-for-TV version of *From Russia with Love* starring James Mason as 007.

The original Ford Mustang was such a success that a bakery near the factory boasted 'our hotcakes are selling like Mustangs'.

Having built its 250 millionth car in the early 1990s, Ford reckons that taken together its cars have between them covered 25 trillion miles. Parked bumper-to-bumper they would reach to the moon and back – twice.

Ford's most powerful road-going Cortina was a Mark IV fitted as standard with a 4.1-litre straight-six for the Australian market.

In 1911 the Ford Model T became the first car to scale Ben Nevis.

It is estimated Ford spent £4,000,000,000 developing the original Mondeo whereas Morgan is reckoned to have designed its best-selling Plus-8 for no more than £13,000.

Peter Stevens whose credits include the Lotus Elan and Jaguar XJR-15 also designed the sunroof handle for the original Ford Granada.

Registering new cars with the DVLA, Ford once accidentally described 14,000 brand new Mondeos as old-fashioned Anglias.

So profitable were UK Ford sales that at its Dearborn HQ, Britain was for some years known as 'Treasure Island'.

Alfa Romeo
Alfa Romeo came first, second, third, fourth, fifth, sixth, seventh, eighth, ninth and tenth in the 1933 Mille Miglia.

In all Alfa Romeo won eleven Mille Miglias and came second another eleven times.

In 1936 the company, believing quality and quantity to be mutually incompatible, managed to build just 10 cars.

The best Alfa engine ever was almost certainly Vittorio Jano's 2.3-litre which won the Mille Miglia three times, Le Mans four times (1931–4), the Targa Florio three times and the 1931 Italian Grand Prix.

The grille for the outrageously beautiful 1954 Giulietta Sprint apparently came off a van, but everything else on it was new and bespoke. The cash-strapped company could afford to do all this because – with the first cars off the line being handed out to the lucky winners – the bulk of the car's design, development and tooling was funded by a national lottery.

Besides being beautiful, the Giulietta won the 1956 Monte Carlo Rally outright and gave several future F1 stars – including double World Champion Emerson Fittipaldi, Jo Bonnier and Jochen Rindt – some of their earliest successes on the track.

FROM WINDMILLS TO PEPPERMILLS: STRANGE KIT TO COME FROM CARMAKERS

Airliner
Ford was the first company in the world to mass produce aircraft, building nearly 200 of its Trimotor airliners in only five years.

Peppermill
Based in Valentigney, in 1842 the Peugeot family began manufacturing a range of coffee, pepper and salt grinders not a few of which can still be bought today.

Typewriter
In 1913, impressed with its quality and integrity, Daimler Motoren Gesellschaft allowed Buromaschinen Werke A.G. of Zella-Mehlis Thuringia to use the Mercedes name on its range of office typewriters.

Ocean Liner
Skoda was once rather grand and in the early days built the Skoda-Hispano-Suiza as well as supplying a number of key components for the *Queen Mary*.

Mechanical Sheep-Shearing Equipment
Wolseley cars were manufactured by a firm founded by Herbert Austin, a spin-off (as it were) from the Wolseley Sheep Shearing Machine Company where Austin had been employed as works manager.

Space Rocket
The solid-fuel motors for the European Space Agency's Ariane rocket were built by a Fiat subsidiary.

Hydroplane
In 1953 Achille Castoldi's record-breaking Arno XI Hydroplane was built around a marinised, much-modified Ferrari F1 engine.

Fighter Jet
Made by Saab, of course, although latterly they used jet engines made by rival Volvo. Bizarrely, when aero-maker Saab diversified into car manufacture in the 1940s the company employed not a single person with any automotive experience.

Jerry Cans
During the Second World War Vauxhall built Churchill tanks, decoy aircraft fashioned from wood and canvas, and, copying the design of the German *wehrmachtskanister*, several million military petrol cans.

Wind Turbines
Both Mitsubishi and Porsche have built wind-powered generators, the first of these dating back to 1940 when the Nazis, desperate to reduce their dependence on imported oil, commissioned the Porsche Type 135 which was capable of producing 130 watts in a stiff breeze.

Double-Decker Bus
In 2008 Aston Martin was declared joint-winner of a competition to provide a modern reinterpretation of the classic double-decker Routemaster – although to date the design has yet to make it onto London's streets.

Racing Car
Rolls-Royce has clearly never had much truck with the somewhat hackneyed maxim that 'racing improves the breed' but the 1963 Marina Andrews Special used a 6.75-litre dry-sump Rolls-Royce V8.

Portable Workbench
The best-selling Black & Decker Workmate was invented by Ron Hickman, an ex-Lotus designer.

Racing Bike
Many car companies started out as cycle makers but Lotus did it the other way round, producing the radical carbon fibre monocoque which at the 1992 Barcelona Olympics enabled Chris Boardman to pedal away with Britain's first cycling gold in nearly three-quarters of a century.

Inflatable Tank
During the war Dunlop manufactured thousands of inflatable rubber Sherman tanks designed to confuse German bombers.

Locomotive Engines
When Ettore Bugatti's splendidly over-the-top Type 41 'Royale' failed to attract sufficient numbers of sufficiently well-heeled buyers, the surplus engines were fitted to a class of rather superior train.

Tractor
Actually, not that unusual: Ferruccio Lamborghini and David Brown of Aston Martin were both tractor magnates long before they got into cars while Harry Ferguson, of 'Little Grey Fergie' fame, was also instrumental in the creation of the world's first high performance all-wheel-drive car, the Jensen FF.

Pasta
Besides his well-advertised designs for the likes of BMW, Ferrari, Oldsmobile, Maserati, Alfa Romeo, Fiat and Volkswagen, in the 1980s Giorgetto Giugiaro designed a new shape of pasta designed to hold more sauce and called *Marille*.

TOYOTAS 'R' US: JAPANESE BUSMAN'S HOLIDAY

The phrase *Yoku manabi, yoku asobe* – 'study well, play well' – is the nearest they have in Japan to our saying about all work and no play making Tanaka a dull boy, and apparently if your day job involves turning out a new car every 20 seconds – which is what Toyota's been doing since August 1935 – the chances are that for relaxation you'll like nothing more than the chance to build another one.

Toyota calls its annual company holiday 'the Idea Olympics', a happy occasion which gives 30,000 factory workers the opportunity to produce and demonstrate creative, original and fun vehicles without a hope that any will ever go into production.

Run as an informal competition for more than 25 years, past highlights have included the wheel-less 'Hazumu' which is designed to shuffle along like a nailbrush across the top of a vibrating washing machine, another one which gets around by using air cylinders and coil springs to jump up and down, and our favourite (the 'Deltabug' or 'Tobleroh-no') which has huge triangular wheels and a top speed of just 6mph. Other favourites include the following:

Hand–Boy

Actually a giant motorised hand, this one moves along by bending its fingers using a unique double four-joint mechanism to claw its way along the tarmac.

Climbing Wallcar

This one mimics animal movements – though not the sort of animal any of us could actually put a name to – and can run, walk or climb by using a second crank axle to move the front wheels separately.

Parent and Child Giraffe

Based on the remains of a Toyota Previa, a fine machine before they started chopping it about, this one gives occupants a 'relaxed tree-top view' by pushing the driver's seat nearly 20ft up through the roof. Ideal for watching sports events you might think, but probably not an air show.

QT Cart

The QT Cart uses a quick-turn changeable angle constant velocity rotating roller transaxle to move forward. Got that?

Hamster Car

As the name suggests, this one is propelled by amplifying the electric power supplied by several on-board rodents running round in wheels. Presumably for a short burst of extra acceleration you just shout out, 'Look out! Freddie Starr is behind you!'

Z-Board

The ultimate skateboard's unique tilting spiral-spring mechanism provides the street-surfer with an environmentally-friendly pollution-free trip – just like a normal skateboard in other words, only it's going faster when you fall off.

Breather

This one certainly has possibilities. Running on pure oxygen, derived from a solution of hydrogen peroxide supplied to a platinum converter, the eco-sounding Breather is a genuine zero-emissions vehicle as are the sleek Sunseeker (which uses twin solar power motors to wind up two sets of powerful elastic bands) and the Hybrid Roller Skate which is recharged by the wearer's own body movements.

THE NAME ATTRACTION: 10 BRANDS REBORN

BMW's new MINI has been such a huge success it's easy to forget the company was taking a risk. Many other once-mighty brands have failed, however, but that hasn't kept others from trying.

Abarth

Abarth means Carlo Abarth, of course, the Austrian-born tuning wizard who from the late 1940s was instrumental in the creation of some outstanding road and race cars. One was a genuine if ill-fated F1 contender called the Cisitalia; others were Simca- and Porsche-based; but mostly Carlo concentrated on producing a range of go-faster Fiat 500s and 850s, the best of which were the original pocket-rockets. With their distinctive scorpion badging they quickly gained a reputation for being true giant-killers while laying the foundations for Italy's 20-year domination of the international rallying scene from 1972 until the early 1990s.

Sadly, by the time Carlo cashed in his chips Fiat had bought him out and was using his name and logo as little more than cosmetic add-ons for its top-of-the-range models. But now it's all change again, with Italy's most illustrious specialist tuning brand in fighting form and relaunched as a separate division operating from its old HQ on Turin's Corso Marche. Leading the charge is the Abarth Grande Punto and the spunky little Abarth 500 Essesse, with the promise of whole range of Abarth-branded cars as well as bits of kit to turn road-going versions into competitive race and rally machines.

Riley

Maybe keen to appease British enthusiasts still reeling from the news that MG-Rover had fallen into foreign hands, Bernd Pischetsreider long ago hinted that BMW might relaunch a number of 'lost' brands including this one. The name eventually only resurfaced in March 2007, however, when *Autocar* reported that William Riley – claiming descent from Percy Riley, who in 1898 built his first car in secret to avoid parental disapproval – wished to build a new, Riley-badged version of the MG SV. A new factory was said to be planned for Blackpool, possibly employing many ex-TVR workers, but at the time of writing the promised carbon-bodied coupé had yet to appear.

Bugatti

The appearance of the EB110 in 1989, and more recently of the monstrous Veyron, understandably upset owners of 'proper' pre-war Bugattis who far from looking for a revival seemed quite happy with their illustrious company grinding to a halt shortly after the departure of its autocratic founder and the death of his son in 1939. It's true too that today's cars lack the purity and elegance of machines such as the Type 13 Brescia and the all-conquering Type 35B. Also their racing pedigree – for decades the defining characteristic of any real Bugatti – although like many Bugattis of old they are, of course, ferociously fast.

MG

With very little fanfare, July 2008 saw the long-awaited announcement about prices for the reborn MG TF roadster. Despite Nanjing Automotive's promise of a 'new look', the new Chinese TF is actually a lot like the old English TF, albeit with prices starting at £16,399 and the original 1.8-litre K-Series Rover engine upgraded to produce 136bhp and meet Euro 4 emissions regulations. Assembled at Longbridge using kits shipped from China, the price for the limited edition LE500 included a relatively high standard specification such as leather seats, piano-black interior trim, parking sensors, an MP3-compatible CD and radio, and a body-coloured hard-top.

Invicta

Surrey-based Invicta built cars from 1925 until 1950, and none finer than the wonderfully caddish 4.5-litre, short wheelbase S-Type whose distinctive 'Low Chassis' design – the frame was under slung at the rear and swept up over the front axle – gave it a look that lay somewhere between Terry-Thomas and Dick Dastardly. In 1931 one drove to victory in the Monte Carlo Rally – only the second time an Englishman had won it – but the depression was a bad time to launch such a machine and in the end only 75 were built of which 68 survive.

In 1982, however, the name reappeared – a Devon-based outfit applying it to the Tredecim, a somewhat ill-proportioned recreation of Jaguar's stillborn XJ13 – and then 20 years later Invicta took flight once more with an all-new coupé called the S1. What its makers described as 'a luxurious Grand Tourer and a no-compromise sports car with the potential to become a class-winning GT racing car,' the S1 was also the first road car ever to feature a one-piece carbon-fibre body shell. Allied to a choice of 4.6- or 5.0-litre V8s supplied by Ford's Special Vehicle Team, early tests at MIRA indicated a 200mph+ top speed.

Lagonda
That most English of marques, Lagonda was actually founded by an American, opera singer Wilbur Gunn taking the name from the Shawnee Indian name for a river and commencing production in Staines in 1906. W.O. Bentley joined after his own company had been taken over by Rolls-Royce, but its reliance on his expensive V12 and numerous post-war supply difficulties led to the troubled company's eventual sale to David Brown's Aston Martin. Despite the guv'nor's fondness for the marque, and customers including HRH the Duke of Edinburgh, it always played second fiddle to the home brand and by 1964 existed in name only. The first attempt at a revival came in 1974, when seven four-door Astons were rebadged as Lagondas. Then, two years later, William Towns created a striking wedge-shape equipped with a wildly futuristic interior and Aston's own 5.3-litre V8. Unfortunately the digital dash never functioned properly, then a period of rabid inflation took the price from a jaw-dropping £24,750 to a thoroughly unsustainable £85,000. By 1996, seven years after the last one was built, a handful were still listed as unsold dealer stock.

Maybach
Alighting from their Citation Xs and mega-yachts, those plutocrats, non-doms and oligarchs who'd sooner not drive themselves can these days opt for a Maybach instead of the more predictable Rolls-Royce – and in 1932 things were not much different. Back then the car of choice would have been Maybach's darkly handsome Zeppelin DS8, which remained in production until 1940 by which time the company had switched to building half-track and tank engines to help the Nazi war effort. With its 8-litre V12 it was every inch the forerunner of today's 57 and 62 *über*-saloons which appeared following the company's revival under more recent Daimler AG management.

Lea-Francis

Originally a bicycle manufacturer (like many early Coventry-based pioneers) Lea-Francis built cars from 1903 until 1952 when the final deathblow was dealt by the imposition of purchase tax on estate cars. Lord Montagu of Beaulieu nevertheless identified the brand's potential as early as 1960, writing in his book *Lost Causes of Motoring*, 'Here is a lost cause which will shortly find itself again.' Sure enough, that October, the new LeaF-Lynx took a bow at Earls Court, although the public failed to warm to the bulbous, purple-and-gold plate 2+2 and none of the three cars which were built found a buyer.

Further attempts at resuscitation followed, the most recent being the 30/230 – indicating 3.0 litres and a top speed 230kph – which made its debut at the 1998 British International Motor Show. A curvaceous if slightly adipose two-seater ragtop, with chassis design and suspension courtesy of Birmingham University's Prof. Jim Randle, the name may have been somewhat optimistic, however. The show car with its bonded aluminium bodywork was actually a non-runner, although plans were afoot to install an uprated version of the 24-valve V6 fitted to the Vauxhall Omega.

Lister

Forever associated with Archie Scott Brown – born without a right hand he nevertheless trounced a succession of Maseratis, Aston Martins and Ferraris – in the 1950s the original Listers used MG and later Bristol engines to great effect thanks in part to advanced aerodynamic designs from the pen of Frank Costin (the Cos in Marcos). Thirty years later the

name reappeared on a succession of 6- and 7-litre Jaguar XJS conversions, and then in 1993 the same outfit unveiled a completely new car called the Storm: four seats, 7.0 litres, 12 cylinders, 594 horsepower – and a choice of road or racing trim.

Spyker

Giving new meaning to the phrase 'going Dutch', Holland's leading supercar and sometime F1 challenger takes its name and logo from a company dating back to 1880 when it was founded by Jacobus and Hendrik Spijker. Their motto – and indeed that of the modern company – was *Nulla tenaci invia est via*, 'for the tenacious, no road is impassable' in Latin. Despite this note of optimism the brothers were declared insolvent by 1925, even though they'd sold nearly a dozen cars to Queen Wilhelmina of the Netherlands and captured the prestigious Double 12-Hour record at Brooklands.

RIPE FOR RENEWAL?
DEAD BUT NOT BURIED (YET)

Shakespeare insisted that 'a rose by any other name would smell as sweet' but clearly the Bard was no petrolhead or he'd have recognised the power of a great name when it comes to shifting product. Of course it seems unlikely that even now anyone's going to launch a car called the SS: William Lyons sensibly dropped that at the start of the war, and Fiat more recently opted to call its faster Abarth 500 the Essesse. Nevertheless the rights to the name are still protected, having been snapped up by Tata together with Daimler, Lanchester and BSA. The Alvis brand has similarly ended up as part of the BAe armaments combine following its abandonment of gentleman's sporting saloons in favour of military hardware.

Dormant Marque	Current Owner
Alpine	Renault-Nissan
Austin	Nanjing Automotive
Auto Union	Volkswagen
Autobianchi	Fiat
Daimler	Tata
Datsun	Renault-Nissan
De Soto	Chrysler

Dormant Marque	Current Owner
DKW	Volkswagen
Glas	BMW
Hillman	Peugeot
Hino	Toyota
Horch	Volkswagen
Hudson	Chrysler
Humber	Peugeot
Imperial	Chrysler
Innocenti	Fiat
La Salle	General Motors
Lanchester	Tata
Morris	Nanjing Automotive
Nash	Chrysler
NSU	Volkswagen
Oldsmobile	General Motors
OM	Fiat
Panhard	Peugeot
Plymouth	Chrysler
Pontiac	General Motors
Prince	Renault-Nissan
Riley	BMW
Saturn	General Motors
Singer	Peugeot
Standard	BMW
Sunbeam	Peugeot
Talbot	Peugeot
Triumph	BMW
Wanderer	Volkswagen
Wolseley	Nanjing Automotive

3

IMPROVING THE BREED

THE A TO Z OF F1

Ayrton Senna: after his death a racing helmet belonging to the star fetched £13,140 at auction in Monaco.

Blood, Sweat & Tyres: More F1 races have been won on Goodyear tyres than on any other brand.

Condoms: The BBC banned the 1976 Race of Champions because the Surtees team was sponsored by Durex.

Day Job: While driving for Ferrari, Mike Parkes moonlighted as a development engineer on the original Hillman Imp.

Engines: One of the all-time greats, the Coventry Climax won three F1 World Championships but was developed from a Government-issue fire pump.

Four-Eyes: Jacques Villeneuve was the first F1 driver to wear contact lenses.

Good Manners: When Stirling Moss crashed his Maserati into a tree in 1956, fellow competitor Fangio stopped and offered him a lift.

Hot Stuff: Racing in temperatures of up to 100°F, Keke Rosberg won the 1984 Dallas Grand Prix wearing a water-cooled skullcap.

Idiot: Impersonating a wild boar while out hunting, the racing driver, land speed record holder and famous Belgian Camille Jenatzy was shot dead by his mates.

Jackie Stewart: Handy behind the wheel, Sir Jackie also won the English, Scottish, Irish & Welsh clay pigeon shooting championships – but failed to make it into the Olympic squad.

Knowing me, Knowing Slim: Tyrrell F1 driver Slim Borgudd used to play drums for Abba.

Lucre: In 1996 the three highest paid sportsmen in the world were all Michaels – Schumacher, Tyson and Jordan.

Mummy's Boy: Enzo Ferrari's mother choked to death on a hard-boiled egg.

Nigel Mansell: Our Nige used to sing to himself during races.

Oops: Alberto Ascari lost the 1955 Monaco GP after accidentally driving into the harbour.

Private Jets: All the drivers have them, but Bernie Ecclestone's got his own airports too, having bought Biggin Hill from the RAF and another one down in France.

Quite Simply the Best: Ferrari is the only team to have contested every F1 World Championship since it began in 1950.

Retirement: After winning the F1 World Championship Jody Scheckter went into business weapons-training police and MoD personnel and is now a farmer.

Smooth Silverstone: With a tolerance of only +/-3mm over 4 metres, the circuit is four times smoother than a newly-resurfaced motorway.

Tobacco: Cigarette companies were for years the sport's biggest sponsors but Emerson Fittipaldi is still the only World Champion to have marketed his own brand of cigars.

Uh-Oh: Riccardo Patrese has pranged more F1 cars than any other driver.

Velocity: Averaging 150.75mph and finishing just 1/100th of a second ahead of the field, Peter Gethin's 1971 Monza win for Yardley-BRM is still F1's fastest and closest drive.

Winning: In 1988 Ferrari triumphed at home in Italy but McLaren-Honda won every other race in that season's F1 calendar.

X-Rated: American racing driver Robert Cowells had the world's first sex-change operation.

Yodelling: Switzerland, Europe's most boring nation, actually banned F1 in 1955 but still has its own racing colours – red with a white stripe.

Zzzzzzz: Only three cars entered the 1926 French Grand Prix. A Bugatti won, another came second and a third one conked out.

THE CIRCUITS

The leading international race series was established in 1950 since when a total of 68 circuits – not all of them purpose-built – have been the venue for official Formula 1 championship races under the auspices of the sport's governing body, the Fédération Internationale de l'Automobile. The following table shows these ranked in order of the number of F1 races they have hosted, the longest circuit being the venue for Italy's 1957 Pescara Grand Prix (with a lap of just over 16 miles) the most famous the Circuit de Monaco, and the most historic – in that it hosted the inaugural 1950 race – Silverstone in Northamptonshire.

Circuit	Grand Prix	Fixtures
Autodromo Nazionale Monza	Italian	58
Circuit de Monaco	Monaco	54
Spa-Francorchamps	Belgian	44
Silverstone	British	42
Nürburgring	German, European & Luxembourg	37
Hockenheimring	German	31
Gilles Villeneuve	Canadian	30
Park Zandvoort	Dutch	30
Autodromo Enzo e Dino Ferrari	San Marino, Italian	26
Autódromo José Carlos Pace	Brazilian	26

Circuit	Grand Prix	Fixtures
Hungaroring	Hungarian	23
Kyalami	South African	21
Autódromo Oscar Alfredo Gálvez	Argentine	20
Suzuka	Japanese	20
Watkins Glen	United States	20
Circuito de Catalunya	Spanish	19
Indianapolis Motor Speedway	Indianapolis 500	19
Magny-Cours	French	18
Österreichring	Austrian	18
Autódromo Hermanos Rodríguez	Mexican	15
Paul Ricard	French	14
Albert Park	Australian	14
Brands Hatch	British, European	14
Autódromo do Estoril	Portuguese	13
Adelaide Street	Australian	11
Reims-Gueux	French	11
Sepang International	Malaysian	11
Zolder	Belgian	10
Autódromo Internacional Nelson Piquet	Brazilian	10
Circuito Permanente Del Jarama	Spanish	9

Circuit	Grand Prix	Fixtures
Long Beach street	United States West	8
Mosport International Raceway	Canadian	8
A1-Ring	Austrian	7
Detroit Street Circuit	Detroit	7
Circuito Permanente de Jerez	Spanish, European	7
Bahrain International	Bahrain	6
Dijon-Prenois	French, Swiss	6
Scandinavian Raceway	Swedish	6
Bremgarten	Swiss	5
Aintree	British	5
Rouen-Les-Essarts	French	5
Shanghai International	Chinese	5
Charade	French	4
Fuji Speedway	Japanese	4
Istanbul Park	Turkish	4
Montjuïc	Spanish	4
Phoenix Street Circuit	United States	3
Prince George	South African	3
Mont-Tremblant	Canadian	2
Caesar's Palace	Caesar's Palace	2
Nivelles-Baulers	Belgian	2

Circuit	Grand Prix	Fixtures
Circuito da Boavista	Portuguese	2
Pedralbes	Spanish	2
Tanaka International	Pacific	2
Ain-Diab	Moroccan	1
AVUS	German	1
Bugatti	French	1
Donington Park	European, British	1
Fair Park	Dallas	1
Marina Bay Street	Singapore	1
Monsanto Park	Portuguese	1
Pescara	Pescara	1
Riverside International Raceway	United States	1
Sebring International Raceway	United States	1
Valencia Street	European	1
Zeltweg Airfield	Austrian	1
Yas Marina	Abu Dhabi	1

Curiously Silverstone also holds the world record for the busiest airport, the heliport at the circuit having documented an incredible 4,200 aircraft movements between dawn and dusk on the day of the 1999 British Formula 1 Grand Prix.

THE WORLD CHAMPIONS

The following table shows the Drivers' World Champion for each season. The parallel World Constructors' Championship was instituted in 1958, the winning marque being shown in brackets only on those rare occasions where this differs from the winning driver's machine.

Season	Driver	Team
1950	Nino Farina	Alfa Romeo
1951	Juan Manuel Fangio	Alfa Romeo
1952	Alberto Ascari	Ferrari
1953	Alberto Ascari	Ferrari
1954	Juan Manuel Fangio	Maserati and Mercedes
1955	Juan Manuel Fangio	Mercedes
1956	Juan Manuel Fangio	Ferrari
1957	Juan Manuel Fangio	Maserati
1958	Mike Hawthorn	Ferrari (Vanwall)
1959	Jack Brabham	Cooper
1960	Jack Brabham	Cooper
1961	Phil Hill	Ferrari
1962	Graham Hill	BRM
1963	Jim Clark	Lotus
1964	John Surtees	Ferrari
1965	Jim Clark	Lotus
1966	Jack Brabham	Brabham
1967	Denny Hulme	Brabham
1968	Graham Hill	Lotus

Season	Driver	Team
1969	Jackie Stewart	Matra
1970	Jochen Rindt	Lotus
1971	Jackie Stewart	Tyrrell
1972	Emerson Fittipaldi	Lotus
1973	Jackie Stewart	Tyrrell (Lotus)
1974	Emerson Fittipaldi	McLaren
1975	Niki Lauda	Ferrari
1976	James Hunt	McLaren (Ferrari)
1977	Niki Lauda	Ferrari
1978	Mario Andretti	Lotus
1979	Jody Scheckter	Ferrari
1980	Alan Jones	Williams
1981	Nelson Piquet	Brabham (Williams)
1982	Keke Rosberg	Williams (Ferrari)
1983	Nelson Piquet	Brabham (Ferrari)
1984	Niki Lauda	McLaren
1985	Alain Prost	McLaren
1986	Alain Prost	McLaren (Williams)
1987	Nelson Piquet	Williams
1988	Ayrton Senna	McLaren
1989	Alain Prost	McLaren

Season	Driver	Team
1990	Ayrton Senna	McLaren
1991	Ayrton Senna	McLaren
1992	Nigel Mansell	Williams
1993	Alain Prost	Williams
1994	Michael Schumacher	Benetton (Williams)
1995	Michael Schumacher	Benetton
1996	Damon Hill	Williams
1997	Jacques Villeneuve	Williams
1998	Mika Häkkinen	McLaren
1999	Mika Häkkinen	McLaren (Ferrari)
2000	Michael Schumacher	Ferrari
2001	Michael Schumacher	Ferrari
2002	Michael Schumacher	Ferrari
2003	Michael Schumacher	Ferrari
2004	Michael Schumacher	Ferrari
2005	Fernando Alonso	Renault
2006	Fernando Alonso	Renault
2007	Kimi Räikkönen	Ferrari
2008	Lewis Hamilton	McLaren (Ferrari)
2009	Jenson Button	Brawn

THE TEAMS

As both car maker and engine manufacturer, the following table of Championship wins shows how Ferrari has continued to dominate the series with only relative newcomer McLaren snapping at its heels.

Team	No. of Championships
Ferrari	15
McLaren	12
Williams	7
Lotus	6
Brabham	4
Cooper	2
Renault	2
Benetton	2
Mercedes	2
Alfa Romeo	2
Tyrrell	2
Maserati	2
BRM	1
Matra	1
Brawn	1

MAD DOGS AND ENGLISHMEN:
FOR ONCE, WE'RE THE TOPS

It's rare these days for British talent to dominate a major sport, and extraordinary to note how at the time of writing the reputations of several rivals – most obviously France and Germany – depend entirely on a single, exceptionally talented driver.

United Kingdom	14	Stewart (3), Clark (2), G. Hill (2), Hawthorn, Surtees, Hunt, Mansell, D. Hill, Hamilton, Button
Brazil	8	Piquet (3), Senna (3), Fittipaldi (2)
Germany	7	Schumacher (7)
Argentina	5	Fangio (5)
Finland	4	Häkkinen (2), Rosberg, Räikkönen
Australia	4	Brabham (3), Jones
Austria	4	Lauda (3), Rindt
France	4	Prost (4)
Italy	3	Ascari (2), Farina
United States	2	P. Hill, Andretti
Spain	2	Alonso (2)
Canada	1	Villeneuve
New Zealand	1	Hulme
South Africa	1	Scheckter

John Surtees is still the only driver to win World Championships on both two and four wheels having competed successfully in both the 350cc and 500cc formulae before switching to cars.

Killed during practice for the 1970 Italian Grand Prix, Jochen Rindt became the sport's only posthumous World Champion although this was not apparent until two more races had been run.

Despite several F1 'families' – the Schumachers, Gilles and Jacques Villeneuve – Graham and Damon Hill are still the only two close relations to each win a Drivers' Championship.

Of those named above Lewis Hamilton, at 23, is famously the youngest ever World Champion – but by no means the youngest Formula 1 driver; Mike Thackwell was only 19 when he drove in the 1980 Canadian Grand Prix.

Fangio was similarly the oldest driver ever to win a World Championship – at 46 – although Louis Chiron is likely to remain the oldest ever Formula 1 driver having been 55 years old when he competed in the 1955 Monaco race.

Fangio is also unique in that he contested the 1954 season on behalf of two different teams, competing in the Argentine and Belgian rounds in a Maserati before transferring to a Mercedes for the remainder of the season.

LIES, DAMNED LIES AND FORMULA ONE

F1's most successful driver ever in terms of the ratio of races entered to races won: American Lee Wallard who entered two races in the early 1950s and managed to win one of them (a 50 per cent success rate compared to Michael Schumacher's 36.4).

F1's least successful driver ever, having lost the most races: Italy's Andrea de Cesaris who entered 214 races, and drove in 208 of them, without winning a single one. In 1986 he started 16 races but managed to finish just twice.

F1's most committed driver: the heroic Rubens Barrichello who by 2009 had entered 277 races, and started 273 of them, but didn't win until his 123rd such race. (Mind you he won the 2000 German Grand Prix despite starting from 18th, an achievement beaten only by John Watson and America's Bill Vukovich.)

Most F1 *Grand Chelems* or grand-slams: still Jim Clark, having managed to take pole eight times before leading the race from start to finish (British Grand Prix '62 and '64, Dutch '63; French '63 and '65; Mexican '63; South African and German '65).

F1's sneakiest driver: Nick Heidfeld, having by early 2009 quietly amassed a total of 206 championship points and 12 podium finishes without winning a single race.

F1's baddest apples: arguably Lewis Hamilton, who was awarded a record five separate penalties in a single season (2008) and his rival Sebastien Vettel who the previous year was clocked speeding in the pitlane just 6 seconds into the start of his Formula 1 career.

THE GREATEST RACE – LE MANS: THE WINNERS

The debate continues as to which is the toughest, truest test of man and machine – the Americans' IndyCar racing which is faster, or international F1 which almost everyone else acknowledges demands more skill of its drivers – but few dispute which is the greatest single race and since 1923 there's never been anything to match the 24 Heures du Mans.

Race Winner	No. of laps completed
1923 Chenard et Walcker Sport	128
1924 Bentley 3 Litre Sport	120
1925 Lorraine-Dietrich B3-6	129
1926 Lorraine-Dietrich B3-6	147
1927 Bentley 3 Litre	137
1928 Bentley 4½ Litre	154
1929 Bentley Speed Six	174
1930 Bentley Speed Six	179
1931 Alfa Romeo 8C 2300	184
1932 Alfa Romeo 8C 2300	218
1933 Alfa Romeo 8C 2300	233
1934 Alfa Romeo 8C 2300	213
1935 Lagonda M45R Rapide	222
1937 Bugatti Type 57G Tank	243
1938 Delahaye 135CS	235
1939 Bugatti Type 57S Tank	248
1949 Ferrari 166MM	235
1950 Talbot-Lago T26	256
1951 Jaguar XK-120C	267
1952 Mercedes-Benz 300SL	277
1953 Jaguar C-Type	304
1954 Ferrari 375 Plus	302
1955 Jaguar D-Type	307
1956 Jaguar D-Type	300

Race Winner	No. of laps completed
1957 Jaguar D–Type	327
1958 Ferrari 250 TR58	305
1959 Aston Martin DBR1	323
1960 Ferrari 250 TR59/60	314
1961 Ferrari 250 TRI/61	333
1962 Ferrari 330 TRI/LM	331
1963 Ferrari 250P	339
1964 Ferrari 275P	349
1965 Ferrari 250LM	348
1966 Ford GT40 Mk. II	360
1967 Ford GT40 Mk. IV	388
1968 Ford GT40 Mk. I	331
1969 Ford GT40 Mk. I	372
1970 Porsche 917K	343
1971 Porsche 917K	397
1972 Matra Simca MS670	344
1973 Matra Simca MS670B	355
1974 Matra Simca MS670C	337
1975 Mirage GR8-Ford Cosworth	336
1976 Porsche 936	349
1977 Porsche 936	342
1978 Renault Alpine A442B	369
1979 Porsche 935 K3	307
1980 Rondeau M379B-Ford Cosworth	338

Race Winner	No. of laps completed
1981 Porsche 936	354
1982 Porsche 956	359
1983 Porsche 956	370
1984 Porsche 956	359
1985 Porsche 956	373
1986 Porsche 962C	367
1987 Porsche 962C	354
1988 Jaguar XJR-9LM	394
1989 Sauber C9-Mercedes	389
1990 Jaguar XJR-12	359
1991 Mazda 787B	362
1992 Peugeot 905 Evo 1B	352
1993 Peugeot 905 Evo 1B	375
1994 Dauer 962 Le Mans	344
1995 McLaren F1 GTR	298
1996 TWR Porsche WSC-95	354
1997 TWR Porsche WSC-95	361
1998 Porsche 911 GT1-98	351
1999 BMW V12 LMR	365
2000 Audi R8	368
2001 Audi R8	321
2002 Audi R8	375
2003 Bentley Speed 8	377
2004 Audi R8	379
2005 Audi R8	370
2006 Audi R10 TDI	380

Race Winner	No. of laps completed
2007 Audi R10 TDI	369
2008 Audi R10 TDI	381
2009 Peugeot 908 HDi FAP	382

MOST SUCCESSFUL MARQUES AT LE MANS

Manufacturer	No. of Outright Wins
Porsche	16
Ferrari	9
Audi	8
Jaguar	7
Bentley	6
Alfa Romeo, Ford	4
Peugeot, Matra-Simca	3
Lorraine-Dietrich, Bugatti, Mercedes-Benz	2
Chenard & Walcker, Lagonda, Delahaye, Talbot-Lago, Aston Martin, Mirage, Renault-Alpine, Rondeau, Mazda, McLaren, BMW	1

TOP NATION:
LE MANS-WINNING DRIVERS' NATIONALITIES

United Kingdom	32
France	26
Germany	14
United States of America	12
Italy	11
Belgium	5
Austria	4
Australia	2
Denmark, Japan, Netherlands, Sweden New Zealand, Argentina	1

LE MANS: LE TRIVIA

During the Second World War the Le Mans circuit served as an RAF airfield but after the fall of France the Germans cleared the site and put up a prisoner-of-war camp.

Traditionally the so-called 'Le Mans start' saw the cars lined up alongside the pit wall, in the order in which they qualified, with the drivers running across the track to their cars at the flag. With occasional pile-ups and fatalities the practice was outlawed following the 1969 race.

This dangerous starting method nevertheless inspired Porsche to locate the ignition key switch to the left of the steering wheel – as it still does today – thus allowing the driver to use his left hand to start the engine while using his right hand to select first gear.

In 1988 a new course record was set by the crew of a WM P88 prototype by taping over the engine openings and hitting 251mph down the Mulsanne straight. Unfortunately the resulting cooling shortfall severely compromised the car's performance elsewhere on the circuit and eventually wrecked the engine.

In 1949, despite never having raced a car before, Norman Culpan took a Frazer Nash to third place and in 1952 Pierre Levegh was the last person ever to attempt to win Le Mans single-handed. After nearly 23 hours behind the wheel he was actually winning, but then his Talbot broke down.

In 1965 Ferraris came first, second and third at Le Mans. The following year Ford, reportedly annoyed at having been pipped at the post by Fiat when it tried to acquire its Italian rival, did it with the GT40.

The smallest car to contest the race was a 569cc Simca Cinq in the 1930s, and the largest an 8-litre Chrysler Viper GTS-R sixty years later. Perhaps the most extraordinary, however, was the 1963 Rover-BMR gas turbine car.

Despite making two attempts the latter was unsuccessful leaving the 1991 Wankel-engined Mazda 787B to claim the prize as the only non-piston engined car ever to win the race. The achievement also stands as the only Japanese Le Mans victory to date.

In 1982 the Belgian driver Jacky Ickx was made an honorary citizen of Le Mans after posting a record six victories in the race. More recently Denmark's Tom Kristensen has beaten him by two (between 1997 and 2008, including six in a row) but in one sense even he can't match Bentley chairman Woolf Barnato whose 1928, '29 and '30 wins mean he is still the only driver to have won Le Mans at every single attempt.

Four-times winner Henri Pescarolo holds the record for the most Le Mans appearances (33) while Japan's Yojiro Terada holds the record for the most starts without a single overall win (29). Britain's Graham Hill is still the only driver to have won the so-called Triple Crown – the Indy 500, Monaco Grand Prix and Le Mans – but he lost when he appeared on TV's *Call My Bluff*.

David Brabham, winner of the 2009 race in Peugeot's historic 1-2 finish, is a former Formula 1 driver and the youngest son of Sir Jack Brabham, Australia's triple F1 World Champion.

THE FULL MONTE

First run in 1911 when the Principality was ruled by Albert I – thereby making it the oldest motorsport event in the world – the 'Monte' is organised each year by the Automobile Club de Monaco which is also responsible for running the Formula 1 Monaco Grand Prix.

The Winners of the Monte Carlo Rally

Year	Winning Driver	Winning Machine
1911	Henri Rougier	Turcat-Mery
1912	Jules Beutler	Berliet
1924	Jacques Edouard Ledure	Bignan
1925	François Repusseau	Renault
1926	Victor Bruce	Autocarrier
1927	M Lefebvre	Amilcar
1928	Jacques Bignan	Fiat
1929	Sprenger van Euk	Graham–Paige
1930	Hector Petit	Licorne
1931	Donald Healey	Invicta
1932	M Vaselle	Hotchkiss
1933	M Vaselle	Hotchkiss
1934	M Gas	Hotchkiss
1935	Christian Lahaye	Renault
1936	L. Zamfirescu	Ford
1937	René Le Bègue	Delahaye
1938	G. Bakker Schut	Ford
1939	Jean Trevoux	Hotchkiss
1949	Jean Trevoux	Hotchkiss
1950	Marcel Becquart	Hotchkiss
1951	Jean Trevoux	Delahaye
1952	Sydney Allard	Allard P1
1953	Maurice Gatsonides	Ford Zephyr
1954	Louis Chiron	Lancia Aurelia GT
1955	Per Malling	Sunbeam–Talbot 90
1956	Ronnie Adams	Jaguar Mark VII
1957	*Event cancelled after Suez Crisis causes fuel shortages.*	
1958	Guy Monraisse	Renault Dauphine
1959	Paul Coltelloni	Citroën ID 19
1960	Walter Schock	Mercedes–Benz 220SE
1961	Maurice Martin	Panhard PL17
1962	Erik Carlsson	Saab 96
1963	Erik Carlsson	Saab 96
1964	Paddy Hopkirk	Mini Cooper S
1965	Timo Mäkinen	Mini Cooper S
1966	Pauli Toivonen	Citroën ID
1967	Rauno Aaltonen	Mini Cooper S
1968	Vic Elford	Porsche 911T
1969	Björn Waldegård	Porsche 911S
1970	Björn Waldegård	Porsche 911S

Year	Winning Driver	Winning Machine
1971	Ove Andersson	Alpine-Renault A110
1972	Sandro Munari	Lancia Fulvia 1.6HF
1973	Jean-Claude Andruet	Alpine Renault 110
1974	*Event cancelled due to Arab Oil Embargo.*	
1975	Sandro Munari	Lancia Stratos HF
1976	Sandro Munari	Lancia Stratos HF
1977	Sandro Munari	Lancia Stratos HF
1978	Jean-Pierre Nicolas	Porsche 911 Carrera
1979	Bernard Darniche	Lancia Stratos HF
1980	Walter Röhrl	Fiat 131 Abarth
1981	Jean Ragnotti	Renault 5 Turbo
1982	Walter Röhrl	Opel Ascona 400
1983	Walter Röhrl	Lancia 037
1984	Walter Röhrl	Audi Quattro A2
1985	Ari Vatanen	Peugeot 205 T16
1986	Henri Toivanen	Lancia Delta S4
1987	Miki Biasion	Lancia Delta HF 4WD
1988	Bruno Saby	Lancia Delta HF 4WD
1989	Miki Biasion	Lancia Delta HF Integrale
1990	Didier Auriol	Lancia Delta Integrale 16V
1991	Carlos Sainz	Toyota Celica GT-Four
1992	Didier Auriol	Lancia Delta HF Integrale
1993	Didier Auriol	Toyota Celica Turbo 4WD
1994	François Delecour	Ford Focus RS Cosworth
1995	Carlos Sainz	Subaru Impreza 555
1996	Patrick Bernardini	Ford Focus RS Cosworth
1997	Piero Liatti	Subaru Impreza WRC97
1998	Carlos Sainz	Toyota Corolla
1999	Tommi Mäkinen	Mitsubishi Lancer Evo VI
2000	Tommi Mäkinen	Mitsubishi Lancer Evo VI
2001	Tommi Mäkinen	Mitsubishi Lancer Evo VI
2002	Tommi Mäkinen	Subaru Impreza WRC
2003	Sébastien Loeb	Citroën Xsara WRC
2004	Sébastien Loeb	Citroën Xsara WRC
2005	Sébastien Loeb	Citroën Xsara WRC
2006	Marcus Grönholm	Ford Focus RS WRC 06
2007	Sébastien Loeb	Citroën C4 WRC
2008	Sébastien Loeb	Citroën C4 WRC
2009	Sébastien Orgier	Peugeot 207 S2000

Unlike grand prix racing and Le Mans the race has also given rise to a film which is actually enjoyable, namely *Monte Carlo or Bust*, the star-studded 1969 sequel to *Those Magnificent Men in their Flying Machines*.

The film starred, among others, Eric Sykes, Terry-Thomas and Gert Fröbe – better known these days as 'Auric Goldfinger' – 007's other rallying connection being his creator Ian Fleming's short stint navigating for 1931 winner, Invicta team driver Donald Healey.

The Hon. Mildred Bruce, wife of the 1927 winner, won the Coupes des Dames the following year, travelled with her husband further into the Arctic Circle than any car had yet been, and at the age of 81 was still looping-the-loop in a De Havilland Chipmunk monoplane.

For many years women were denied the chance to enter, and for a number of years the Rally even included a subsidiary prize called the Late Public Schools MC Cup for the best performance by a former public schoolboy. Another cup for the most comfortable car entered was won on several occasions by an otherwise wholly uncompetitive Bentley.

In 1952 the Englishman Sydney Allard became the first man to win the event in a car of his own design – a P-Type saloon powered by a flathead Ford V8 – finishing ahead of new boy Stirling Moss driving a Talbot. Sydney's achievement has never been repeated.

The winner the following year was Gambong-born Maurice Gatsonides, who also built cars – fewer than a dozen of them – but with little success. He had more luck with his invention of the technically clever but widely despised 'Gatso', the roadside speed-camera with which all motoring enthusiasts are today familiar.

Winning the event in 1964, '65 and '67, the giant-killing Mini Cooper S also won the 1966 race before being disqualified on the most minor technicality – the wrong kind of headlights – thereby enabling the organisers to claim a 'local' victory for a Paris-based Finn driving a Citroën.

In 2009, during the running of an alternative 'green' Monte which is not expected to replace the official event, an electric Tesla Roadster managed to cover 241 miles on a single charge to beat a plug-in Porsche 911 and a handful of Mitsubishi iMiEVs.

NATIONAL RACING COLOURS

Distinguishing colours were first introduced in 1900, the occasion being the first truly international race – the Gordon Bennett Trophy, named after the *New York Herald* proprietor who devised the event. At that time the colour green – considered by many on the continent to be a lucky colour – was awarded to Charles Jarrott to compensate for his drawing unlucky 13 as his number. Over time a new system was devised, the details of which are shown below.

Country	Body	Bonnet (if different)
Argentina	Blue	Yellow
Australia	Green	Gold
Austria	Blue	
Belgium	Yellow	
Brazil	Pale yellow	
Bulgaria	Green	White
Canada	White and green stripes	
Chile	Red	Blue
Cuba	Yellow	Black
Czech Republic	White	Blue/white
Denmark	Silver-grey	
Egypt	Pale violet	
Finland	White	Blue stripes
France	Blue	
Germany	Silver or White	
Greece	Pale Blue	White stripes
Hungary	White/Green	Red
Ireland	Green with orange band	
Italy	Red	
Japan	Ivory	Red disc on bonnet

Country	Body	Bonnet (if different)
Jordan	Brown	
Luxembourg	Red, white and blue stripes	
Malaysia	Yellow	White
Mexico	Gold	
Monaco	White with red stripe	
Netherlands	Orange	
New Zealand	Green and silver	
Philippines	Red and Blue	Yellow
Poland	White	
Portugal	Red	
South Africa	Gold	Green
Spain	Red	Yellow
Sweden	Blue bottom, yellow top	
Switzerland	Red	White
Thailand	Pale blue with yellow horizontal band	
United Kingdom	Green	
United States	White with blue stripes	
Uruguay	Pale blue with large red band	

REGRETS, I'VE HAD A FEW

In 2009 a number of well known names were asked about any significant gaps in their motorsport education.

'I'd love to have done more in F1. I grew up a child of the Scalextric era, passionate about cars such as the March and JPS Lotus. Imagine lining up on a '70s Formula 1 grid alongside the likes of James Hunt, Mario Andretti and Emerson Fittipaldi. I reckon the social scene was pretty extraordinary then too.'
Mark Blundell, Formula 1, sports car, and CART driver

'I've driven many of Jaguar's finest racing cars from E-Types, the XJS touring cars throughout Europe, and the sublime Le Mans and Daytona 24-hour winning masterpieces. I've even driven the Jaguar F1 car at Silverstone and through Regent Street, London, of all places! A 1950s D-Type at Le Mans would have completed the set nicely.'
Martin Brundle, Formula 1 driver and race commentator

'I wish I could have raced an old 1937 Auto Union: it had power unequalled until turbocharged F1 GP cars in the '80s; or to have enjoyed both racing and the camaraderie of the Bentley Boys in the Le Mans 24-hour races of the 1920s. I had the privilege of practising driver changes with Woolf Barnato's extraordinary aviator daughter Diana, before she sadly passed away aged 90: imagine if I'd got her to actually race with me!'

Tom Kristensen, eight-times Le Mans champion

'I'd love to have driven a Maserati T60 Birdcage on its first outing, and enjoyed the astonishment of fellow competitors at its performance. I'd also love to have driven the Ferrari GTO at Le Mans in 1962, maybe driving it from Maranello to the circuit to run it in!'

Nick Mason, musician and historic racing car driver

'I remember thinking, when the XK120 was launched, how amazing it was for such a beautiful car to have twin overhead camshafts, 120mph top speed and only cost £1,000. The XK was so far ahead of its time and definitely the car to have. I was very keen to race one, especially after the 120's win in its first race at Silverstone in 1949. I managed to borrow one the year after and win the TT, which was my big breakthrough.'

Sir Stirling Moss, still most commonly referred to as 'the greatest driver never to win a world championship' . . . which must be annoying for him

'The early '70s was probably one of the coolest eras to race in: drivers showed their personalities as well as the cars. I watched a film showing the 1972 Maserati and Ferrari sports cars battle from Sebring to Le Mans to Watkins Glen: those cars were so stylish and sexy to look at, and I'm sure fun to drive as well.'

Allan McNish, multiple American Le Mans Series and
Le Mans champion

STRAIGHT ON RED:
THE WORLD LAND SPEED RECORD

The early land speed record cars were battery-powered, Camille Jenatzy's sleek, cigar-shaped *La Jamais Contente* – the name means 'never satisfied' – becoming in 1899 the first vehicle ever to travel at more than 100kph (62mph). The next landmark was Louis Rigolly's run in 1904 when he managed to exceed 100mph.

Leon Serpollet's vaguely ovoid steam car (it was actually nicknamed the Oeuf de Pâques, or Easter Egg) was the first non-electric car to capture the World Land Speed Record after its run along Nice's Promenade des Anglais in 1902. Electric cars soon reasserted their dominance, however, although the first road vehicle to hit 200kph (124mph) was another steamer.

In 1906 the ladies' record fell to Miss Dorothy Levitt who chalked up a speed of 96mph in a Napier at Blackpool to win the title of 'Fastest Girl on Earth'.

Kenelm Lee Guinness at Brooklands was the last man to break the LSR on a race track, and Ernest Eldridge in his 1924 Fiat Special the last to set such a record on a public highway.

Sir Henry Segrave's Sunbeam Tiger was similarly the last genuine racing car to break the record — thereafter only highly specialised one-off machines were up to the job – while Sir Malcolm Campell's 1927 run at Pendine Sands in South Wales was the last time the record was broken on European soil.

Sir Malcolm Campbell's series of Bluebirds were named after the 1908 stage play by his friend the Nobel laureate Maurice Maeterlinck. Years later his similarly speed-mad son Donald turned down the chance to officially open the Chiswick Flyover and his place was taken by Hollywood starlet Jayne Mansfield.

John Cobb's Railton Mobil Special was the final record-breaker to use driven wheels – in other words the last actual LSR 'car' as opposed to a jet- or rocket-powered projectile. Its best official result was just over 393mph for a standing kilometre although it managed to hit 400mph momentarily.

Some attempts over the years have also been remarkably cost-effective: the aptly named Green Monster, Art Arfons' multiple record breaker, reportedly cost only £6,000 to build.

Britain's Andy Green, current Land Speed Record holder, RAF Tornado pilot and Cresta Run aficionado, got the job of ThrustSSC driver after answering an advertisement in the newspaper.

Year	Driver	Car	Speed (mph)
Electric			
1898	Gaston de Chasseloup-Laubat	Jeantaud Duc	39.24
1899	Camille Jenatzy	CGA Dogcart	41.42
1899	Gaston de Chasseloup-Laubat	Jeantaud Duc	43.69
1899	Camille Jenatzy	CGA Dogcart	49.93
1899	Gaston de Chasseloup-Laubat	Jeantaud Duc	57.65
1899	Camille Jenatzy	*La Jamais Contente*	65.79

Year	Driver	Car	Speed (mph)

Steam-Powered

Year	Driver	Car	Speed (mph)
1902	Leon Serpollet	Gardner–Serpollet	75.06
1906	Fred Marriott	Stanley Rocket	127.66
2009	Charles Burnett III	BSCC Inspiration	151.085

Internal Combustion Engined

Year	Driver	Car	Speed (mph)
1902	W.K. Vanderbilt	Mors Z Paris–Vienne	76.08
1902	Henri Fournier	Mors Z Paris–Vienne	76.6
1902	M. Augières	Mors Z Paris–Vienne	77.13
1903	Arthur Duray	Gobron Brillié	83.46
1903	Arthur Duray	Gobron Brillié	84.73
1904	Arthur Duray	Gobron Brillié	88.76
1904	Louis Rigolly	Gobron Brillié	94.78
1904	Henry Ford	Ford 999 Racer	91.37
1904	Pierre de Caters	Mercedes Simplex 90	97.25
1904	Louis Rigolly	Gobron Brillié	103.56
1904	Paul Baras	Darracq Gordon Bennett	104.53
1905	Arthur MacDonald	Napier 6	104.65
1905	Victor Hémery	Darracq V8 Special	109.65
1909	Victor Hémery	Benz No 1	125.94
1914	L.G. Hornstead	Benz No 3	124.09
1919	Ralph DePalma	Packard 905	149.875
1922	Kenelm L. Guinness	Sunbeam 350HP	133.7
1924	René Thomas	Delage La Torpille	143.21
1924	Ernest Eldridge	Fiat Mephistopheles II	146.01
1924	Malcolm Campbell	Bluebird	146.15
1925	Malcolm Campbell	Bluebird	150.86
1926	Henry Segrave	Sunbeam Tiger Ladybird	152.3
1926	J.G. Parry-Thomas	Higham-Thomas Special	171.01
1927	Malcolm Campbell	Bluebird II	174.88
1927	Henry Segrave	Sunbeam 1000hp	202.98
1928	Malcolm Campbell	Bluebird III	206.95
1928	Ray Keech	White Triplex	207.55
1929	Henry Segrave	Napier Golden Arrow	231.56
1931	Malcolm Campbell	Bluebird	246.08
1932	Malcolm Campbell	Bluebird	251.34
1933	Malcolm Campbell	Bluebird	272.46
1935	Malcolm Campbell	Bluebird	276.16
1935	Malcolm Campbell	Bluebird	301.129
1937	George E.T. Eyston	Thunderbolt	312

Year	Driver	Car	Speed (mph)
1938	George E.T. Eyston	Thunderbolt	345.2
1938	John R. Cobb	Railton Special	350.06
1938	George E.T. Eyston	Thunderbolt	357.33
1939	John Cobb	Railton Special	369.74
1947	John Cobb	Railton Mobil Special	393.82

Turbojet/Turbofan Powered

1963	Craig Breedlove	Spirit of America	408.312
1964	Tom Green	Wingfoot Express	415.093
1964	Art Arfons	Green Monster	434.356
1964	Craig Breedlove	Spirit of America	468.719
1964	Craig Breedlove	Spirit of America	526.277
1964	Art Arfons	Green Monster	544.134
1965	Craig Breedlove	Spirit of America	555.485
1965	Art Arfons	Green Monster	572.546
1965	Craig Breedlove	Spirit of America	600.842
1983	Richard Noble	Thrust2	633.468
1997	Andy Green	ThrustSSC	760.343

Rocket-Powered

1970	Gary Gabelich	Blue Flame	630.389

4

TOP CARS FOR TOP PEOPLE

NOT ALL ROLLS AND DAIMLERS: THE ROYALS AND THEIR CARS

Although the aristocracy were foremost in promoting the early car, the Royals took slightly longer to join the rush. At their head Queen Victoria reportedly loathed all cars, finding the smell of 'these very shaky and disagreeable conveyances exceedingly nasty.' George V similarly declared the new Lanchester Forty to be 'more suited to a prostitute than a prince,' and once alighting from a Rolls-Royce compared it to a rabbit hutch. Similarly it wasn't until the 1950 Silverstone Grand Prix that a reigning sovereign – George VI – went to watch a motor race despite this country's obvious ability in that arena.

In fact even now most royals seem to prefer watching horses going round in circles to cars – famously the AA's millionth member, the Princess Royal only qualified for her HGV licence so she could drive a horsebox – which is why it came as a bit of a surprise when the programme for the 1997 Grand Prix Historique de Monaco listed Prince Charles

among the entrants. It later transpired that the driver in question was actually one Charles Prince, driving a Maserati 300S, but looking down the following list one can see that what Prince Phillip terms 'the Firm' has owned a few interesting machines over the years.

1906 Renault 14/20hp XB

The first car to be owned and run by a British Royal, Edward VII took the plunge after enjoying a run in a steam-powered machine owned by chocolatier chum Gaston Menier. Clearly enthusiastic about his new purchase – a year later he bestowed the coveted Royal prefix on the new Automobile Club – he was nevertheless not remotely interested in how they worked. While a bit more clued up about this than his cousin Kaiser Wilhelm (who believed cars were powered by 'potato spirit'), His Majesty would literally growl at his chauffeur every time his Hooper-bodied car in its Royal Claret livery broke down or misbehaved.

1934 McLaughlin-Buick

Unaware of Mrs Simpson's affair with a car salesman – the truth about this only came out in secret government papers which were released in 2003 – Edward VIII liked cars a lot and was the first British sovereign to drive himself regularly. In 1934 he ordered a customised, Canadian-built McLaughlin-Buick which was finished in gleaming black and still owned by him at his abdication two years later. The limousine included such refinements as drinks and jewellery cabinets, vanity mirrors, luncheon trays and even a set of blinds to shield him from the public when he was out and about with the double-divorcée. Dubbed the 'most romantic car in the world' it survived and in December 2007 was sold for $185,000 at auction in the US.

1935 Standard Nine

While he was later to be seen tooling around in a variety of more exotic machines, the Duke of Edinburgh – or Prince Philip of Greece as he then was – began his motoring life in one of these, a cheap and cheerful little runabout which is reckoned to have saved the Standard Motor Company because its larger cars weren't selling at all well. In 1950 the company had another brush with royalty when, during a demonstration for Princess Margaret at the Motor Show, the chairman Sir John Black pulled the wrong lever and accidentally incinerated his company's sole example of its advanced, alloy-bodied TRX prototype.

1960 Nash Metropolitan

An extraordinary attempt to scale down what was then *the* look in American auto design, the Nash Metropolitan with its trademark two-

tone paintjob ended up looking more like a bath toy than anything approaching a real car. Despite this, and notwithstanding its feeble performance, it racked up a number of famous owners, including Elvis Presley, Paul Newman and Alma Cogan. Princess Margaret had one too, given to her as a wedding present, but unfortunately the black convertible was stolen while she was out to lunch. After a police chase through the streets of London, a 14-year-old schoolboy was arrested.

1965 Ogle Triplex GTS
A precursor to the fashionable if flawed Reliant Scimitar GTE, the genuinely one-of-a-kind Triplex GTS advanced the use of glass in automotive aerodynamics and pioneered the concept of the sports estate. Oil billionaire Nubar Gulbenkian apparently offered Ogle a blank cheque for it, Lord Snowdon was photographed climbing into it, and when Prince Philip let it be known that he would find the so-called Glazing Test Special a good daily driver, arrangements were made for him to borrow it for the next two years. Clearly his daughter was impressed too, and given a Scimitar for her 20th birthday she was later apprehended after proceeding in it with undue haste.

1967 Mini
En route to becoming Britain's first royal university graduate, in October 1967 – when the Mini was definitely the car to be seen in – Prince Charles arrived at Trinity College, Cambridge, in a red chauffeur-driven example.

1974 Aston Martin Lagonda

Prince Charles has been seen in a variety of Aston Martins too, including this ultra-rare Lagonda. Essentially a stretched, four-door version of the company's popular V8 saloon, the idea appealed enormously to company boss and Lagonda fan David Brown but only seven were completed before the project was canned in 1976. With an extra 11in in the wheelbase the ride was much better than the standard car, but it remained somewhat unwieldy with a mammoth 45ft turning circle.

2002 Bentley State Limousine

After decades as a royal favourite, Daimler was edged out of the Royal Mews by Rolls-Royce, and eventually similar treatment was meted out to that company too when Bentley's new owner, Volkswagen, presented Her Majesty with a pair of bespoke Bentley State Limousines to mark her Golden Jubilee. Longer, taller and wider than the Arnage on which it is based, it features suicide doors – 'Coach doors' in Palace parlance – armoured bodywork, armoured glass, run-flat tyres and a mine-resistant floor. The price has never been revealed because there are absolutely, positively and most definitely no plans to offer the model for general sale.

2002 Audi allroad quattro

It caused a bit of an uproar in the press when the Prince of Wales did a deal with Audi instead of buying British, but presumably with all the big British brands having gone to the wall or been bought out by foreign concerns he just couldn't see himself being driven around town in a Ginetta or strapping himself into a Noble. According to a St James's Palace spokeswoman at the time 'Vauxhall have decided to stop making Omegas so he has had to pick another car.' In fact he ordered a matched pair of these for himself and his Duchess and Audi, clearly delighted, admitted, 'This deal is worth its weight in gold. The Prince is probably our most important customer.' Probably?

2006 Land Rover Defender

In the 2006 film *The Queen*, Helen Mirren was shown in the title role driving a Defender through the Scottish countryside. When the vehicle breaks down fording a river the queen quickly set to work to sort it out, commenting 'I was a mechanic during the war,' in reference to her time in the Auxiliary Territorial Service which is where she learned to drive. She really does drive Landies too, and despite being the only person in the country who can legally drive cars without a number plate she has got one – JGY 280 – which George VI gave to her on her 18th birthday.

RULING PASSIONS:
PRINCES, POPES & POTENTATES

Tsarina Alexandra
Although she never actually took the controls – heaven forefend! – the wife of the last Tsar took delivery of a De Dietrich in 1898 with hubby Nicholas II later ordering a bespoke Delauney-Belville limo for himself. This was equipped with a massive 11.65-litre engine and no fewer than eight pedals and in 1901 the Imperial family also commissioned from Adolphe Kégresse a new kind of vehicle designed to work in the snow. The result, delivered a year later, is thought to be the world's first practical tracked vehicle.

Alphonso XIII
Passionate about cars and a skilled driver, before the First World War the Spanish monarch was a patriotic supporter of the Hispano-Suiza company one of whose cars – the winner of the 1910 Coupe de l'Auto – was renamed in his honour: the Alphonso-Hispano.

Leopold II
In 1901 the King of the Belgians ordered from the prestigious Parisian firm of Rothschild et Cie an elegant, curvaceous new body for his new Mercedes, the actual form of the resulting coachwork still being known today as a 'Roi des Belges'.

Mohammad Reza Shah Pahlavi

The self-styled 'King of Kings', the last Shah of Iran issued an imperial edict to Maserati after admiring a picture of a 3500GT in the company's catalogue and recognising at once such a splendid personage as himself obviously needed something even faster. The result was the outstanding 5000GT, possibly the finest roadgoing Maserati of all time, and when he saw it King Saud of Saudi Arabia thought he'd better have one too.

King Farouk

The last king actually to rule over Egypt, and well known for his uncontrollable self-indulgence, Farouk once ordered a new Bentley but was too fat to climb in it by the time he took delivery. In 1952, widely considered as corrupt as he was ineffective, he and his son were packed off into exile complaining that soon there would be only five kings left: 'of spades, diamonds, clubs, hearts – and of England.'

Fateh Jang Nawab Mir Osman Ali Khan Siddiqi

Besides the inevitable gold fittings and throne, the Nizam of Hyderabad, Asaf Jah VII, had his Rolls-Royce equipped with gold lace curtains, gold brocade upholstery and a solid silver cupola on the roof. Fitted with fairy lights, this enabled the owner to glance up and see something akin to the night sky twinkling above his head – something he clearly did only very rarely as the car reportedly covered fewer than 350 miles before he tired of it and moved it on.

Hassanal Bolkiah Mu'izzaddin Waddaulah

Besides a jet aeroplane with gold-plated furniture and a palace with nearly 1,800 rooms, the Sultan of Brunei has a car collection variously

estimated at between 3,000 and 6,000 cars. These include five McLaren F1s, a brace of bespoke Ferrari 456GT saloons, and two six-door Rolls-Royce Silver Wraiths which at 20ft 6in are the longest ever produced.

Pius XII

An early 'popemobile' was Pius XII's magnificent Cadillac V16. Mae West and Al Capone each had one too, although it seems unlikely the three ever met to compare notes. One of his predecessors, Pius X, had been gifted an Itala as early as 1909 but for reasons of his own refused ever to ride in it.

Thubten Gyatso

At the time his country's only motorist and more formally known as Ngawang Lobsang Thupten Gyatso Jigdral Chokley Namgyal, the thirteenth Dalai Lama owned two little Austin Sevens which he had registered as TIBET 1 and TIBET 2.

Maharaja of Patiala

After more than 100 years, Lieutenant-General His Highness Farzand-i-Khas-i-Daulet-Inglisha Mansur-i-Zaman Amir-ul-Umra Maharaja Dhiraj Rajeshwar Shree Maharaja-i-Rajgan Maharaja Sir Bhupindra Singh Mohinder Bahadur Yadu Vanshavatans Bhatti Kul Bhushan Maharaja Dhiraj of Patiala is still the longest name on record of any Rolls-Royce owner. He had 38 of the famous British cars in all, at one point using several of them as dustcarts after a spat with the factory, and was said to spend £31,000 a year on underwear with his pants coming in at £200 a shot.

SOMETHING NAZI IN THE WOODSHED: DICTATORS AND THEIR DAILY DRIVERS

Lenin

Vladimir Ilyich Ulyanov, better known to the world as Lenin, founded the Russian motor industry but had a thing about English cars and – reluctant to allow his socialist principals to get in the way of his personal preferences – ordered no fewer than nine Rolls-Royces for his own use.

Stalin

His successor, however, could see the political value of a locally-sourced limo and had a factory in Leningrad (now St Petersburg) reinterpret some of the larger Buick and Packards of the day. With production of these so-called ZIS and ZIL cars later moving to Moscow, his own heavily armoured version weighed in at something approaching 7.5 tons.

Mao

The Chairman was also keen to control the means of production, and after examining a visiting ZIS ordered the Changchun No.1 Automobile Factory to do to Chrysler what ZIS and ZIL had already done to Packard and Buick. Complete with ivory switchgear, expensive walnut trim and gaudy satin tapestry upholstery, the result he called the Hongqui Red Flag.

Mussolini

A keen motorist, and a lover of Alfa Romeos even before he came to power, Mussolini particularly favoured the lavish V8 Astura models and commissioned a special cabriolet version from Pininfarina. When he fell from power he fled Italy in a Fiat, but was quickly captured and together with his mistress was strung up by his heels.

Hitler

Just as there are said to be more bits of the true cross in existence than would ever have been needed, so it is that ownership of just about every surviving 'Grosser' Mercedes is attributed to Hitler. Certainly he was a fan of these, ordering his first in 1924 and requesting that the floor of a later 770K version be made 5in higher in order to increase his stature. With 2in bullet-proof glass as standard, his parade vehicles typically weighed around 8,000lbs but were still good for 100mph – although somewhat hypocritically the Führer ordered the death penalty for anyone else who was caught speeding.

Hirohito

Hitler's wartime ally was also a big fan of the 'Grosser', and in the absence of a domestic manufacturer capable of creating anything close in terms of appearance or quality, the Japanese Emperor ordered a total of seven armoured Mercs before the Axis finally collapsed.

Franco

In the 1950s Rolls-Royce built just 18 examples of its heavyweight Phantom IV having let it be known that none would be sold to anyone except British royals and foreign heads of state. An impressive 17 have survived – including a brace of limousines and a bullet-proof cabriolet ordered by the Spanish generalissimo – the only one lost being that ordered by the equally unsavoury, Maserati-fancying Shah of Iran.

Trujillo
The Dominican dictator favoured Ghia's Chrysler Crown Imperial, his fellow customers including Juan Péron and Indonesia's President Sukarno. Eventually production of these shifted to Spain, at which point Franco ordered a couple for himself – reportedly at a cost of a million pesetas apiece – which soon took the lead in his typically bombastic 14-car motorcades accompanied by up to 16 police outriders.

Tito
Like Mussolini, the Yugoslav leader Josip Broz Tito was a bit of a petrolhead, worked for a while as a mechanic in the Austro-Daimler racing team and later drove himself around in his Ghia-bodied Cadillac Eldorado or a specially-bodied Fleetwood convertible. When he died in 1980 his personal collection included a pair of armoured Mercedes 600s, a Rolls-Royce Phantom V, two pre-war models – a Horch and a Packard Super 8 – and a ZIS with one previous careful owner, Marshal Stalin.

Ceausescu
Besides the inevitable Mercedes-Benz 600 Pullman, the Romanian communist leader had a Buick Electra which was a gift from President Nixon. Also a host of lesser vehicles including a Peykan and a Dacia 2000, the first of these being an Iranian-built Hillman Hunter and the second a Renault 20-based hatchback reserved for senior Party members. Lucky guys.

Rasputin
Not quite a dictator, perhaps, but in pre-Revolutionary Russia he certainly wielded an unhealthy influence. When everyone had had enough of this (and of him) he took his last ever ride in a Rolls-Royce after being fed enough cyanide to kill a dozen men, shot several times, and viciously clubbed as he lay dying in the snow. Still not quite dead, he was eventually dropped through a hole in the ice of the frozen River Neva.

WHEN THE PEASANTS REVOLT:
10 COOL CLASSIC MILITARY VEHICLES
IN WHICH TO ESCAPE

1914 Rolls-Royce Silver Ghost
Lawrence of Arabia called it 'fighting de-luxe' when he and his men used three Rolls-Royce Silver Ghosts to obliterate two enemy command

posts, blow up a bridge, wipe out almost an entire cavalry regiment and destroy many miles of railway. Recognising their incredible durability, the idea of an armoured Ghost had come from Bendor, 2nd Duke of Westminster, who donated 12 of his own cars to the cause and would have agreed with Lawrence that 'all the Turks in Arabia could not fight a single Rolls-Royce armoured car in open country. They were worth hundreds of men to us in these deserts.'

Soon yet more rich and titled owners were handing over their cars, among them Lord Rothschild who later proved Lawrence's claim that it was 'almost impossible to break a Rolls-Royce' when he wielded a sledge-hammer to stop his own falling into enemy hands. Churchill immediately spotted the potential of a new species of armoured 'land ship' and with the expertise of leading Admiralty designer Captain Eustace Tennyson D'Encourt scores of Ghosts were soon kitted out with reinforced axles, more than 3 tons of ⅜-inch armour plating, a crude but tough 5ft diameter steel-cylinder turret and a devastatingly effective Vickers-Maxim machine gun.

1942 DUKW

Vauxhall at Luton built decoy aircraft to fool enemy bombers, in the US Ford eventually put aside its founder's misplaced admiration for Hitler and built more than 8,600 Liberator bombers, and General Motors went into business building 'Ducks', the distinctive six-wheeled amphibious jeep-thing. In military parlance the D in DUKW indicated a vehicle designed in 1942, the U stood for utility, the K denoted that it was all-wheel drive and the W referred to its powered, paired rear axles.

Proving ideal for rapid beach landings under fire in the Mediterranean, the Pacific, during the D-Day invasion of the Normandy beaches, and in countless other 'ops' throughout the 1940s, more recently the super-durable craft have been used by abalone fishermen in California and for rescuing people hit by Hurricane Katrina in 2005. Also to show tourists a different side of London courtesy of The London Frog Company which operates a fleet of eighteen bright yellow amphibians, two of which once raced down the Thames with Sir Stirling Moss and Jenson Button at the controls.

1940 M2/M3 Half-track

Suitable for the widest possible range of applications – from gun carriage to armoured personnel carrier, from an air defence role to go-anywhere bridge-builder – the M-family of half-track vehicles was developed following the US Army's evaluation of the pioneering Citroën Kégresse. Built by a number of different manufacturers, including White, International Harvester and the Diamond T Motor Car Company, in all more than 41,000 units went into battle with many forming part of the US Lend-Lease programme whereby rich America allowed poor Europeans to have the pick of their kit on the never-never (providing they were on the right side, obviously).

1939 Daimler Dingo

With submissions from Alvis, BSA and Morris for a light, fast, 4x4 reconnaissance vehicle, in 1938 the War Office awarded the contract to Daimler (then part of British Small Arms or BSA) to build what is now recognised as one of the best armoured vehicles of the entire war. Officially called the Scout Car – the Dingo name came from Alvis – 30mm armour and a Bren gun mount gave reassurance to the two-man crew, while an ingenious pre-selector gearbox with a fluid flywheel provided five speeds in either direction. Lancia sneakily cloned the design in 1943, which therefore saw action on both sides of the war.

1942 VW Type 128/166

Still the world's most popular amphibious vehicle, the iconic Schwimmwagen used drivetrain and other components from the VW Types 82 and 87, an early four-wheel drive Kübelwagen prototype and the four-wheel drive Kommandeurwagen or staff car. That's sufficient to make it a kissing cousin to Ferdinand Porsche's original Beetle, the Type 60 KdF Wagen – short for *Kraft durch Freude*, the name of the leisure wing of the Nazi organisation meaning 'Strength through Joy' – although Erwin Komenda, Porsche's body designer, redesigned its tub as the flat underside of the civilian car made it unstable at speed through water.

Powered by a 1,131cc air-cooled boxer engine, the Schwimmwagen developed around 25 horsepower at 3,000rpm and was equipped with a screw-type propeller which dropped down at the back to adapt it to ocean-going mode. (As the front wheels doubled up as twin rudders, the steering wheel remained the principal means of control when the vehicle did this.) By 1944 more than 15,500 Schwimmwagens had been built – 133 of them at Porsche – but while around 130 are known to have survived barely a dozen of these are in original, unrestored condition.

1940 Willys Jeep

Designed and delivered in a mere 49 days to meet the urgent requirement of the US Quartermaster Corps for a compact, rectangular quarter-ton truck with all-wheel-drive, after driving the first prototype the test driver Major Lawes hit the nail on the head when he climbed out of the little 2.2-litre machine and declared, 'I believe this unit will make history.' Too true: by 1945 nearly 640,000 of them had gone to war, the name being derived from its official designation (GP, or General Purpose) and the fact that a well known cartoon character of the time went by the name of 'the Jeep'.

The troops loved them too, the magazine *Special-Interest Autos* noting, 'for thousands of soldiers the Jeep was the nearest thing to a sports car they had ever driven: roadster body, bucket seats, fold-down windscreen, quick steering, tight suspension, snappy performance. Everybody wanted one.' But of course they were needed elsewhere at this time and, seeing service on literally every front, Jeeps were soon employed as gun-mounts and rocket launchers, ambulances, troop carriers, staff cars, amphibians and even rail cars. Its contribution to the Allied victory was quite literally incalculable and – capable, tough and uniquely versatile – it's still quite simply the best.

1940 Universal Carrier

Invariably referred to as a Bren Gun Carrier, even when not equipped as such, the UC was designed by Vickers and went on to become the most ubiquitous armoured vehicle in British history. Initially there were many different types offering a wide range of different applications, but with the benefits of standardisation obvious to the wartime economy, these were eventually reduced to just one model, hence the 'Universal' tag. Powered by an 85hp Ford V8 mounted amidships, the 3.75 tonner was good for a respectable 30mph and with a range of 150 miles quickly proved its worth to the Allied Forces.

1941 Scammell Pioneer

Dating back to the 1920s, a time when the Empire needed tough, strong haulers to operate where metalled roads were far from usual, the Pioneer was invaluable in wartime for transporting goods over rough or broken ground. More than anything its combination of a suspension set-up with plenty of movement, a strong, low-revving Gardner 6-cylinder diesel and the ability to maintain traction in most conditions gave it huge pulling power. Allied to a low-load trailer the Pioneer quickly found a role as the tank transporter *par excellence* and later, in peacetime, many found employment moving carnie folk and their kit around the country.

1938 Humber Super Snipe

With a well-earned reputation as the 'poor man's Rolls-Royce' and powered by a 4.1-litre 6-cylinder engine producing around 85hp, the definitive wartime staff car was good for nearly 80mph which was outstanding for its day. Among the many commanders who used them, the most notable was Kennington-born Field Marshal Bernard Law Montgomery KG GCB DSO. He used his throughout his campaigns in North Africa and Europe but in 1944 ditched 'Old Faithful' in favour of a Rolls-Royce Silver Wraith – mindful perhaps of his imminent elevation to the peerage.

1959 Alvis Stalwart

Owing nothing to the supremely elegant 3.0-litre saloons built by the company during this same period, the 6x6 Stalwart was a development of earlier military vehicles such as the Saracen APC, Saladin armoured car and Salamander fire tender. Within its waterproof hull, power came

from a 220hp Rolls-Royce B.81 giving it a top speed of 43mph on land and 5 knots on water. Its suitability for assuming the role of what the brass-hats refer to as a high-mobility load-carrier was never in doubt thanks to an ability to climb over 45cm obstacles and cross trenches up to 1.5m wide. Wicked looking too.

CARS WITH DODGY WARTIME CONNECTIONS

Volkswagen Beetle
The idea for a German people's car came from Hitler but the design belonged to Ferdinand Porsche who aided the Nazi war effort with a number of other designs including the Tiger Tank, the V1 'doodle-bug' flying bomb, an ingenious amphibious off-roader, and a 26-ton self-propelled howitzer.

Renault 4CV
Born near Prague and buried in Austria, Ferdinand Porsche was technically a Czech, not a German. Considered too small a fish to fry at Nuremburg, he was nevertheless locked up by the French in 1945 and put to work helping Renault perfect its wonderful little four-door saloon.

Auto Union Type 22
Today among the most valuable racing cars in the world, 16-cylinders, 6.3 litres and 550bhp made a fine Grand Prix car and an effective record-breaker. Like so many of the 'Silver Arrows', however, it lives on in infamy having raced with a swastika on its flanks although these are not infrequently airbrushed out in promotional pictures used today.

Mercedes–Benz 540K *Spezial Roadster*
Nicknamed the Blue Goose, and an exemplar of pre-war German engineering, this very particular smoky-blue two-seater was 'liberated' by the 101st Airborne Division of the US Army in 1945 having previously been the personal transport of Reichsmarschall Hermann Goering. Described as 'used government surplus' it was auctioned off for $2,167 in the 1950s, but if sold today would almost certainly fetch several thousand times that amount.

WOULD YOU BUY A CAR FROM THIS MAN?

Speaking of dictators, the motor industry has had a few of its own over the years, the reality being that it's nearly always these guys who come up with the best stuff. Just think about it, and about how often we moan about cars these days. How they're all being created by committee, designed by computers, engineered in a way to suit bean counters rather than buyers, blah blah . . . and why is it that we can't go back to the good old days when truly great cars sprang from the fertile minds of extraordinary individuals?

Hang on – extraordinary individuals? Surely that's just another way of describing a megalomaniac, because whatever else you think the likes of Henry Ford, Enzo Ferrari, Ettore Bugatti and even our own revered Walter Owen Bentley were up to it certainly wasn't pandering to the wishes of the public. Instead this sort invariably displayed a single-minded determination – which is to say a certain bloody-mindedness – to visualise the future, devise a means of getting there, and then see it through to completion. It's like Fiat's Gianni Agnelli used to say: it is a good idea to have an odd number of directors on the board, but 'three's too many'.

Today, for example, photographs of Henry Ford show him with that wry little half-smile and a positive twinkle in his eye, looking every bit like the sort of benign, generous benefactor who would voluntarily choose to pay his workforce double what his rivals paid theirs. The reality of course is that he did this knowing that his workers would spend it all on new cars – which they did, so he got his money back again – and that until 1921 his control over his workforce was so strong that he even insisted that no Ford worker ever spend so much as a cent of it on the demon drink.

Old Henry was clever, no question – by the end of the First World War half of the cars in the entire world were Model-Ts – but to get a true measure of the man you need to read his own, private newspaper, *The Dearborn Independent*. Run with the express purpose of campaigning against Jews, it showed him to be a committed anti-Semite who blamed them for all manner of ills – including short skirts and jazz music – so much so that today Ford enjoys the dubious distinction of being the only American citizen to be mentioned by name in Hitler's *Mein Kampf*.

In Italy Enzo Ferrari was honoured by fascists too, Mussolini bestowing on him the title *Commendatore* although there's no evidence that, like

Ferdinand Porsche, he provided comfort or material support to fascists. He certainly ruled like a dictator, however, every inch a self-confessed monomaniac who hired and fired top racing drivers like they were nobodies. Then as now no-one ever described Sr. Ferrari as nice and indeed it's often been observed by those fortunate enough to have visited Maranello in his heyday that Ferrari employees at all grades had a tendency to walk as if on eggshells to avoid incurring the old man's sudden outbursts of wrath.

By contrast, over the border, Ettore Bugatti was clearly quite popular with his workers, and even knew them all by their first names. Something else he knew was that he was right – about everything – modestly christening his first child L'Ebé after his own initials and insisting all his shoes were made with separate compartments for the big toes. Refusing to build any cars with left-hand drive, and opposing the introduction of numerous technological advances (including front-wheel brakes and independent front suspension) he finally flounced out of the factory when his workers went on strike in 1936 – and simply never came back.

And so to Bentley, and the great W.O. who at first insisted these new-fangled motorcars were 'disgraceful vehicles that splashed people with mud' but then changed his mind after trying one for himself. Like Bugatti he's generally described as a good employer, although it was said that if he found a youngster in the plant doing something he didn't like he would, like the fabled basilisk, fix them with a stare so penetrating that they'd never grow another inch.

Unfortunately as an employee he was even worse. Moving to Lagonda after his bankrupt company was taken over by Rolls-Royce, W.O. was dismissed when the owner heard 'he would sit in a car for an hour or so, puffing his pipe, and then say "we must raise the dashboard one inch" only to put it back the way it was later.' After that he designed a new 3.0-litre engine for Armstrong-Siddeley, but unfortunately that company too decided that it was better off without his talents and W.O. slipped into retirement with his third and final wife.

TOFFS ON WHEELS

In the 1920s the composer and diplomat Lord Berners had a piano built into the back of his Rolls-Royce.

On April Fool's Day 1968 the Duke of Bedford was banned from driving for six months after being seen 'undertaking' another car on the M1. Police identified him by his number plate, DOB 1.

Prince Borghese, victor of the original 1907 Peking-Paris race, was related by marriage to Napoleon.

Field Marshall Sir Henry Wilson (1864–1922) conceived such a violent dislike of taxis that when on leave in London he would prowl the streets in his Rolls-Royce looking for cabs he could force onto the pavements.

Earl Mountbatten of Burma's number plate was LM 0246, the four digits being the peer's ex-directory Mayfair telephone number.

A keen pilot, the Old Etonian racing driver Prince Bira of Siam fitted his glider with extra windows so that his pet dog could come up and admire the view.

Charles Chetwynd-Talbot, otherwise the 23rd Lord Shrewsbury, is the only earl to have a make of motor car named after him. The cars themselves were initially manufactured at Ladbroke Grove in west London.

After colliding with another car in 1961 Lord Derby successfully escaped prosecution by claiming that his view had been restricted by the long bonnet of his Rolls-Royce.

The bigamous Earl Russell, brother to philosopher Bertrand Russell and a fierce defender of motorists' rights, queued all night in 1904 to obtain the first ever car registration plate: A1.

The Rt. Hon. John Theodore Cuthbert Moore-Brabazon, later Lord Brabazon of Tara, owned the first car in England with metallic paint. A pale blue Aston Martin, the unusual paint effect was said to have been discovered by accident when the ball bearings in a paint-grinding machine broke up.

Lord Howe took up motor racing between the wars at the suggestion of a magistrate who was fed up fining him for speeding. Subsequently his performance in a 1.5-litre Delage at Brooklands was never surpassed, and driving with Captain Sir Henry 'Tim' Birkin Bt. he won Le Mans in an Alfa Romeo.

Possibly the highest ever price for an old Cortina, in 1995 the racing baronet Sir John Whitmore sold his 30-year-old car for a staggering £34,642.

Goodwood Festival of Speed founder Lord March, heir to the Dukedoms of Richmond, Gordon, Lennox and d'Aubigny used to work for film director Stanley Kubrick.

No shrinking violet, Lord Kitchener had his Rolls-Royce painted bright yellow in order that he would be instantly recognised when driving around London.

An early President of the Automobile Association also favoured bright yellow, the 5th Earl of Lonsdale ordering his domestic staff into yellow livery and insisting his gardeners paint their wheelbarrows and watering cans a similar hue. It was also on his watch that the extraordinary decision was taken to make the Nazi Joachim von Ribbentrop an honorary member of the Association.

Lonsdale's opposite number – at the Royal Automobile Club in Pall Mall – was the old Duke of Sutherland who used to keep the engine of at least one of his four Rolls-Royces running at all times in order that he could make a quick getaway should he so wish.

A fellow duke, in July 1922, set off from London in another Rolls-Royce, His Grace the 7th Duke of Leinster having entered into a wager requiring him to drive to Aberdeen in under 15 hours in order to win a hefty £3,000 from a friend.

SALOONER THE BETTER: SUPERCARS FOR THE CHAUFFEUR-DRIVEN CLASSES

1958 Facel Vega Excellence
Persuaded by a French government desperate for something locally-built that was prestigious enough for the President, Facel Vega stretched its existing chassis and stuck in an extra set of doors. Unfortunately the car's pillarless construction looked elegant but did tend to sag in the middle if all four doors were opened at the same time.

1963 Lagonda Rapide
Based on an Aston Martin DB4, not that you would know it to look at it, and markedly less successful with just 55 sold during the four years it was in production.

1963 Maserati Quattroporte
In its day the world's fastest four-door saloon, 679 Quattroportes were built with examples going to Peter Ustinov, the Aga Khan and, er, Soviet leader Leonid Brezhnev, champion of downtrodden peasants everywhere.

1967 Iso Fidia
Boasting the world's biggest windscreen apparently – who worked that one out? – but a 5.7-litre V8 made the Fidia yet another victim of the 1973 fuel crisis.

1970 De Tomaso Deauville
Despite crude Ford V8 power and slightly derivative Jaguar XJ6 looks, the car found 244 buyers including both the London Saatchis.

1971 Monica
Inspired by the Facel Vega, powered by Chrysler and named after the owner's wife, 13mpg did for it in the face of the 1973 Arab Oil crisis.

1971 Monteverdi 375/4
Swiss, crisply styled and exceptionally elegant, but Peter Monteverdi failed to lure Europe's jet-set away from their Mercedes 600s and in the end barely 50 were sold.

1977 Aston Martin Lagonda
Radically-styled and with a space-age interior, the first one broke down during a press photo call and while it limped on for more than 12 years, sales never really recovered.

1978 Lamborghini Faena
A Frua-bodied forerunner of today's hideous Estoque concept of which, fortunately, just one was built.

1980 Ferrari Pinin
Built to mark Pininfarina's 50th anniversary, and the best-looking of the lot, the world wasn't yet ready for a Ferrari saloon car and it has remained a one-off.

TEN CELEBRITY SUPERMODELS: THE MOST EXPENSIVE CARS EVER AUCTIONED

For a number of years now the most valuable sales have been private ones, transacted away from the glare of publicity, with rumours still circulating that more than a decade ago a Japanese enthusiast paid an incredible $14 million for a Ferrari 250 GTO. Confirming such sales is sadly nigh on impossible, but the following list – all priced in dollars, for ease of comparison – shows the highest prices to date which have been paid on the open market.

1957 Ferrari 250 Testa Rossa – $12.2 Million
In May 2009 RM Auctions' Ferrari Leggenda e Passione sale in Maranello smashed all existing records with one of 22 pontoon-fendered sports racers, its beetle-black body combining an incredible racing history with breathtaking looks, fantastic performance and handling, and outstanding, unrestored condition.

1961 Ferrari 250 GT SWB California Spyder – $10.9 Million
Ex-James Coburn, this 1961 model was also sold by RM Auctions, at a previous Ferrari Leggenda e Passione sale hosted by the Ferrari factory.

1931 Bugatti Royale Kellner Coupe – $9.7 Million
One of just six built – two of which make it into this list – the Type 41 Royale was sold in 1987 during a Christie's auction at the Royal Albert Hall in London. (The early date certainly needs bearing in mind when comparisons are made with the two more recent sales of Ferrari.)

1962 Ferrari 330 TRI/LM Testa Rossa – $9.2 Million
The last Ferrari competition car to have its engine in the front, this particular machine was driven by the late Phil Hill and Oliver

Glendebien at Le Mans in 1962. The sale was held by RM in 2007, again at the factory.

1937 Mercedes–Benz 540K *Spezial Roadster* – $8.2 Million

Formerly part of Bernie Ecclestone's collection, and assumed to be the finest surviving example of the company's outstanding 5.4-litre sports car, the price was achieved during an RM sale at Battersea Park, London, in 2007.

1929 Mercedes–Benz 38/250 SSK – $7.4 Million

Another exceptional sporting Mercedes – the name comes from *Super Sport Kurz*, meaning short – the SSK is one of thirty-three built and was sold by Bonhams in Sussex in 2004.

1904 Rolls–Royce 10hp – $7.25 Million

The highest price ever paid for a Rolls-Royce (and for a pre-1905 car of any make) the occasion was Bonhams' annual London Olympia Motoring Sale in December 2007.

1931 Bugatti Royale Berline De Voyager – $6.5 Million

Once part of Bill Harrah's incredible 1,400-strong collection, this second Type 41 was auctioned in Reno, Nevada, at a glittering 'Evening Royale' in 1986.

1962 Ferrari 250 GTO – $6.2 Million

Sold at a Las Vegas car auction in 1991, the occasion marks the last time a Ferrari 250 GTO was sold in an open sale rather than behind closed doors.

1953 Ferrari 340/375 M Berlinetta Competizione – $5.8 Million

The winner of the 1954 Le Mans 24-hour endurance race, and so clearly one of the most important Ferrari racing cars ever offered for sale, the 340/375 was sold in 2007 at an RM Auction held at the Ferrari factory.

5

CELEBRITY ENDORSEMENTS

BABY YOU CAN DRIVE MY CAR:
THE BEATLES AND THEIR MINIS

A knowledgeable motoring enthusiast and keen follower of F1, George Harrison bought a Mini Cooper S in 1965, commissioning coachbuilder-to-the-stars Harold Radford to strip and rebuild the car before painting it blacker than black. Later, with the psychedelic movement in London reaching a peak, the car was treated to a more colourful paintjob and after a brief appearance in the film *The Magical Mystery Tour* it was sold to Eric Clapton. Harrison reportedly regretted the sale, however, and bought the Mini back at a later date to have it restored.

In 1965 Paul McCartney's car of choice was another Radford Cooper S, this one painted a special shade of Aston Martin metallic green with a number of other modifications including A-M taillights, a black leather interior, a larger-than-usual sunroof and super bright headlamps.

Rumoured to have bought his first Mini before he had even learned to drive – possibly as a present for first wife Cynthia – John Lennon later had it rebuilt by Radford as an *über*-luxurious Mini de Ville and was photographed driving it to Abbey Road Studios following the death of Brian Epstein. Lennon also had a Phantom V limo which he painted to look like a trippy fairground ride – a psychedelic treatment Rolls-Royce sniffily described as 'unfortunate' – and when the Fab Four were awarded MBEs he famously returned his insignia to Buckingham Palace in the back of a white Mercedes-Benz 600 Pullman.

Keen not to be left out, Ringo Starr's 1966 Mini was originally coachbuilt by Hooper for Epstein but when Ringo took it on he had it rebuilt again (this time by Radford, whose hatchback conversion meant there was room in the back for Ringo's drums). He had a Facel Vega too, but after crashing it was persuaded to sell it by John, Paul and George on the grounds that three Beatles would be no good without the fourth.

AND THE REST ...

With echoes of mad Basil Fawlty giving his Austin 1100 a damned good thrashing, when Elvis Presley's rare De Tomaso Pantera failed to start one morning he pulled out a handgun and shot it. (Like Led Zeppelin's manager Peter Grant, the King had several of his cars fitted with concealed compartments for guns.)

Janis Joplin modestly had her Porsche 356 Cabriolet covered all over with images of, er, Janis Joplin. Liberace similarly spent an incredible $600,000 gold plating his 1931 Cadillac, but even with mink carpets it later failed to reach even a tenth of the price at auction.

Keith Richards of the Rolling Stones bought a rare and valuable Nazi staff car, but then accidentally demolished it on the day he took delivery. He also had a Bentley S3 Flying Spur fitted with Turkish Embassy flags to fool the police into thinking he had diplomatic immunity – The Who's Keith Moon merely had his fitted with a throne in the back – while fellow Stone Charlie Watts owns a rare 1938 Bugatti even though he reportedly never drives.

David Crosby of close-harmony hippie combo Crosby Stills Nash & Young famously learned to steer with his knees enabling him to freebase with a hand-held blowlamp. And after swallowing enough LSD to drop an ox, the late Jim Morrison of The Doors liked to drive his hopped-up Mustang down railway tracks just for a laugh.

Rod Stewart claims he quit The Faces to go solo so that he could earn the £1,000 he needed to buy a Marcos GT, while American rocker Jon Bon Jovi once settled for a second-hand Morgan rather than join the then-lengthy queue to buy a new one.

And finally here's a question for you: is Sting, self-styled saviour of the South American rainforest, the same Sting who once appeared in the TV ad for the gas-guzzling Jaguar S-Type?

CELEBRITY ENDORSEMENTS

The first celebrity ever busted for bad driving was almost certainly film actor and director Harry Myers who picked up a speeding ticket in 1904 after doing 12mph in a 10mph zone in Dayton, Ohio.

Closer to home Princess Anne was once fined £400 and awarded five penalty points after admitting to driving her Bentley at 93mph on a dual carriageway in Gloucestershire. This was by no means her first offence.

Mel Gibson was similarly put on probation after insulting the arresting officers who clocked him drink-driving at 87mph in a 45mph zone.

El Hadji Diouf, sometime Bolton Wanderer, pleaded guilty to a charge of drink-driving in December 2005.

In 2006 the model Caprice lost an appeal against a ban imposed after she had been caught and breathalysed on Tottenham Court Road.

Rowan Atkinson has been caught speeding in one of his Aston Martins, and crashed another into a barrier while racing in Yorkshire in 2001.

Slow-hand, heavy-foot: in 2004 ageing rocker Eric Clapton was banned from driving in France after being caught doing 134mph in a Porsche 911 Turbo near Merceuil.

Poor old Jerome Flynn was caught doing 85mph in 2004 and failed to avoid a ban despite arguing that he'd be teased if he was banned and had to catch the bus.

In 2007 Paris Hilton was gaoled for three weeks after driving her Bentley across LA without lights while on probation for drink-driving.

Ben Affleck was once done for doing 114mph on a 70mph interstate in the state of Georgia.

After being found slumped over the wheel of his Range Rover in 2006, George Michael pleaded guilty to a charge of being unfit to drive through drugs.

Al Gore was fined after the inconvenient truth emerged that he'd been seen speeding in his Toyota Prius. So much for being green. . . .

Former footballer and BBC Five Live pundit Steve Claridge once claimed he was only doing 100mph because he was desperate to find a loo.

Former Newcastle United striker Obafemi Martins was fined £550 (with £400 costs) after being caught doing 106mph in his Porsche Cayenne.

Golfer Colin Montgomerie was once fined £835 for driving his Bentley at 70mph in a 40mph zone. It wasn't his fault: he told the police, 'this car is too quick.'

Prince Naseem Hamed, a boxer, was gaoled for 15 months after crashing into another car at 90mph and leaving the scene.

Film director Oliver Stone was bailed after being arrested for drink-driving and drug possession at a police checkpoint on Sunset Boulevard.

In January 2005 footballer Rio Ferdinand was banned after overtaking a marked police car and averaging 105.9mph on a 2-mile stretch of the M6.

Olympian Amir Khan was banned from driving in October 2007 and then again in January 2008 after running a red light, knocking down a pedestrian and driving at a speed in excess of 70mph.

Arrested in May 2007 the rapper Trevor Smith – who prefers to be known as Busta Rhymes – pleaded guilty to a drink-driving charge.

A month after being caught at 83mph in a 70mph zone, and with nine points on his licence already, Chris Tarrant was clocked doing 60 in a 40 zone and banned for six months.

Herbie Fully Loaded star Lindsay Lohan, apparently pretty loaded herself, was gaoled for 83 minutes after admitting drink-driving and cocaine charges.

Sometime boxer Chris Eubank has twice been arrested for illegally parking a lorry outside Downing Street.

In 2007 the chef Gordon Ramsay crashed an off-roader while using it to herd water buffalo.

Kiefer Sutherland was gaoled in December 2007 after making an illegal U-turn while driving under the influence.

After being clocked at 104mph, computer whizzkid and Apple co-founder Steve Wozniak claimed he was confused by the difference between miles per hour and kilometres per hour. The judge wasn't having any of it.

In 2007 footballer Milan Baroš had his Ferrari confiscated by French police after being clocked at 168mph.

That same year Brooke Shields crashed into a house after attempting to drive while wearing a pair of high platform shoes.

The comedian Patrick Kielty has twice been caught driving at speeds in excess of, having once been clocked at 121mph in a 60mph zone.

Anne Robinson was banned from driving in 2008 after a camera recorded her doing 43mph in a 30 zone.

England rugby player Mike Tindall has twice been banned for drink-driving.

After running a police roadblock in October 2005 actress Stockard Channing was arrested, breathalysed, fined and made to attend an alcohol-education course.

The orchestral conductor Oscar Levant once defended a charge of being caught speeding on the grounds that one 'can't possibly hear the last movement of Beethoven's seventh and go slow.'

Finally, and as recently as May 2009, Tom Riall, boss of the speed camera company Serco, pleaded guilty to speeding after doing more than 100mph on an A-Road.

NO PUBLICITY PLEASE: CELEBRITY NUMBERPLATES

The queen doesn't have to have one at all, and the Lord Provosts of Edinburgh and Glasgow get the use of S 0 and G 0 respectively. The rest of us mostly get what we're given, although publicity-shy sportsmen, singers and other showbiz types have traditionally paid extra to stand out from the crowd.

MB 1
Max Bygraves – crooner

MAG 1C
Paul Daniels – conjuror

COM 1C
Jimmy Tarbuck – professional Liverpudlian

H41 RDO
Nicky Clarke – hairdresser

MR D1Y
Tommy Walsh – TV house-fixer-upper

JOK IE
Mike Read – comedian

1 LAF
Bernard Manning – comedian

EH 1
Engelbert Humperdinck – singer

S8 RRY
Robbie Williams – singer

AMS 1
Lord Sugar – TV entrepreneur

CHU 8B
Chris Tarrant – TV presenter and keen angler

RYM 4N
Theo Paphitis – Ryman's proprietor and TV entrepreneur

D1 DDY
David Hamilton – DJ

6 HEF
James Martin – chef

SM 7
Sir Stirling Moss – retired racing driver

CR 7
Cristiano Ronaldo – expensive soccer player

UK VIN
Vinnie Jones – ex-soccer player

UK TAN
Vinnie's missus, Tanya.

SLIP ME A GRAMME: CELEBRITY BAD HABITS

In 2008, in a bid to highlight the green credentials of car clubs and car-sharing, one operator, City Car Club, produced a hall of shame of gas-guzzling celebs and published for each of them an estimated average pollution measure based on the cars they were known to own and drive and the CO_2 produced.

1. Simon Cowell – 457g/km average, from a stable which includes a Bugatti Veyron, Ferrari F430 and Rolls-Royce Phantom.

2. Jay Kay – 444g/km average, from a stable which includes a Ferrari Enzo and Rolls-Royce Phantom.

3. David Beckham – 421g/km average, from a stable which includes a Bentley Arnage and Continental GT, a Hummer H2, and a Lamborghini Gallardo plus sundry off-roaders and Mrs B's Porsche 911.

4. Rowan Atkinson – 398g/km average, from a stable which includes a McLaren F1, V8-engined Mercedes E500 and an Aston Martin DB7.

5. 50 Cent – 394.5g/km average, from a stable which includes a Rolls-Royce Phantom and a couple of bullet-proof limos.

6. Rio Ferdinand – 379g/km average, from a stable which includes the usual footballer line-up of a Bentley Continental GT and BMW X5 with a monstrous Cadillac Escalade thrown in for good measure.

7. Steven Gerrard – 361g/km average. Another footballer, so . . . Bentley Continental GT, BMW X5, Aston Martin Vanquish and Porsche 911 Turbo.

8. Kerry Katona – 359.5g/km average, from a stable which includes a Lamborghini Gallardo, Aston Martin Vantage, Range Rover and 911 Turbo.

9. Wayne Rooney – 308g/km average, from a stable which includes the inevitable Vanquish, X5 and 911 Turbo together with a Mercedes-Benz CLK.

10. Justin Timberlake – 287g/km average, from a stable which includes a Range Rover, a Jeep Wrangler, and an Audi TT.

Perhaps the only surprise is that none of them drives a Dodge Viper SRT-10, rated by the Environmental Transport Association as the Least Green Car 2009 with its 8-litre engine pumping out so much CO_2 in a single year – a Cowell-busting 488g/km – that to absorb it would require a full acre of mature oak forest, equivalent to 322 individual trees.

MACHINES FOR DRIVING: WHY FAMOUS ARCHITECTS SHOULDN'T DESIGN CARS

On the one hand it seems bizarre that architects, concerned with large stationary objects, should be interested in designing moving ones. On the other, Le Corbusier famously described his houses as 'machines for living' and as an exercise in miniaturised architecture a car is perhaps little more than a room-on-the-move. A sort of compact mobile environment encompassing everything architects profess to love – art, design, and the very latest in new technology – the only problem being that most of them come up with such ridiculous ideas.

Frank Lloyd Wright (1867–1959)
Who but an architect, you might ask, would have proposed building a vehicle out of reinforced concrete, or one with leather curtains and semi-circular windows? The latter was the brainchild of the AC-owning Frank Lloyd Wright, his intention being to echo the horizon with the hemispherical sky above. His 1955 'Road Machine' was even madder, relying on a sort of ballbarrow arrangement at the front end with one driven wheel on the off-side and an appearance strangely reminiscent of a nineteenth century Hansom cab.

Le Corbusier (1887–1965)
Despite accepting the deposit on a 1925 Voisin 10 CV as part-payment for a set of architectural drawings, 'Corb' – real name, Charles-Edouard Jeanneret – wasn't much of a driver but like so many of his colleagues he thought he could do better than the professionals when it came to designing anything. What he called his *Voiture Minimum* managed to wow the arts establishment in 1928 but by the time he had finished working on the design a decade later it looked somewhat primitive alongside Dr Porsche's VW Beetle – not least because he'd completely ignored such minor trifles as suspension and the means of propulsion.

Walter Gropius (1883–1969)
Compared to Wright's barmy proposals those produced by the Bauhaus founder at least looked like normal cars, and indeed his proposal to fit seats to a 1931 Adler which folded down into couchettes supports the theory that he was literally designing a miniature house on wheels. In fact he got the commission as a friend of the family which owned the Adler company, although more recently it has been suggested that he was only brought in as a design consultant as part of a wily marketing ploy to attract buyers to what was otherwise a rather dated range of cars.

Joseph Emberton (1889–1956)
The designer of the innovative, steel-framed Piccadilly store Simpson's (and London's Olympia 2 exhibition centre), Emberton designed the Lancia Lambda Airway. Taking his inspiration for this from the Alcock and Brown's trans-Atlantic Vickers Vimy bomber, he gave the car's strange wooden 'fuselage' a steeply raked windscreen and fitted wicker seats, an altimeter and even an airspeed indicator. His bulbous three-window dormer at the rear was said to be exceptionally aerodynamic, but was never put to the test.

Norman Bel Geddes (1893–1958)

Like many others, Bel Geddes persisted in the belief that a teardrop was the most aerodynamic shape, his 'Car No.9' being a vast, eight-wheeled behemoth that was so large it would have dwarfed a Winnebago. He insisted a flying version was also a possibility, but fortunately none of his clients stumped up the money for a working prototype.

Carlo Mollino (1905–73)

A rare exception in that his design not only looked good but actually worked, Mollino's imaginative Osca-based Nardi *Bisiluro* ran at Le Mans but retired before the 24 hours were up. The name, meaning Double Torpedo, accurately describes this diminutive 750cc projectile whose excellent aerodynamics were achieved by having the driver sit low down in one torpedo-like wing with his weight being offset by the engine located in the other. Happily the car survives, and is on display in Milan's Leonardo da Vinci Science Museum.

Jan Kaplicky (1937–2009)

The pessimistic Czech's NatWest Media Centre at Lord's is one of London's most elegant contemporary buildings, and as the world's first semi-monocoque building (it looks like the nose-cone of a Formula 1 car) it won the 1999 RIBA Stirling Prize. He also won praise for his wacky Selfridge's offshoot in Birmingham's Bull Ring, but his design for a caravan is something else altogether being beautifully reminiscent (from outside) of a Henry Moore sculpture but cramped inside with little actual space for the occupants to move around.

Buckminster Fuller (1895–1983)

The granddaddy of them all, however, is probably Buckminster Fuller whose pioneering geodesic dome inspired Blair's ill-fated southbank folly and who first turned his hand to automobile design back in the 1930s. He too fell for the myth of the teardrop, and applying it to the concept of an economy car – that's what he called it – he drew a quite absurd machine, seating four abreast but requiring six wheels and no fewer than three separate, highly complex air-cooled five-cylinder radial engines.

His later Dymaxion safety car was if anything even crazier, and not just because he actually built and drove several of them around New York with author H.G. Wells. Six metres long and large enough to seat ten or eleven, the Dymaxion had only three wheels, channelling the considerable power of its 3.6-litre Ford V8 through the single one at the rear. It also relied on the same one wheel for braking and steering, but was at least relatively aerodynamic.

Driven by Al Williams, a famous stunt-pilot in his day, the prototype was reported to have hit 120mph when tested in July 1933, although that now seems unlikely given the rear wheel's tendency to lift off at anything over 50. Delighted nonetheless, Fuller pronounced it the safest car ever built – but then it crashed, and with fatal results.

Perhaps the final word on the subject should be left to the late French philosopher and cultural commentator Roland Barthes, who on seeing the then-new Citroën DS described it as 'the exact equivalent of the great Gothic cathedrals: the supreme creation of an era, conceived with passion by unknown artists, and consumed in image if not in usage by the whole population which appropriates them as a purely magical object.' Or to put it another way: cars are clearly much too important to be left to an architect.

GILDED LILIES: WHY FASHION DESIGNERS SHOULDN'T DESIGN CARS

For many years the temptation to pair fashion designers with automotive brands has proved too strong to resist. It's true that some designers have had a genuine interest: Ralph Lauren's immaculately restored collection includes several rare Bugattis, pre-war Bentleys and Alfas, as well as a Ferrari 250 GTO and McLaren's F1. Mary Quant similarly lauded the Mini as 'a handbag on wheels. It went exactly with the miniskirt, was optimistic, exuberant, young, flirty, looked fantastic and did everything one wanted.' But when they have a go at designing one themselves, it nearly always ends in tears.

In the 1970s the (now defunct) American Motors Corporation launched several designer specials in a bid to gee-up sales. Bizarrely quite collectable, these included the Hornet Sportabout Wagon, with green and red striped upholstery by Gucci, also a Matador sedan styled by Oleg Cassini, and a Javelin SST fastback with a garish interior by Pierre Cardin and a large, thirsty V8 just in time for the fuel crisis. Weirder still however, was AMC's 1973 Levi's Gremlin which – as if the name wasn't bad enough – offered discerning buyers denim seats with copper rivets, yellow stitching, even the trademark orange Levi's tab.

Once in while, however, things work out a little better for all concerned. In the late 1990s Toyota devised a bright yellow version of one of its slower-selling coupés, giving it swoopy green stripes and a name – the Paseo Galliano Special Edition – which must have kindled in the public's imagination an association with the talented British designer.

Similarly when Paul Smith was asked to design a funky Mini he took his cue from a distinctive colour scheme he had employed in a previous season and gave the car a jazzy makeover with 84 stripes in 26 different colours before it went on display in Tokyo. Clearly this particular paintjob was much too complex to put into production, but it spawned a pair of limited edition Minis which did go on sale featuring 'exclusive' bonnet, boot and grille badges with their glove boxes, boots and engine bays finished in a vibrant citrus green. Nice.

More recently the same designer tried his hand at striping a Jaguar X-Type as well – the finished car being auctioned at a charity bash attended by the likes of Elton, Kylie and Sting – while Fiat produced a funkier-than-normal version of its little city car called the Seicento 2Tone. This was unveiled at Michiko Koshino's flagship London store, the designer using one of the cars to negotiate the narrow streets of Soho to get there.

By far the wildest to date, however, is Matthew Williamson's unique take on the Rover 25. Remember them? Designer by appointment to all the usual suspects – Elizabeth Hurley, Kate Moss, Jade Jagger, Madonna, blah-blah – his modifications to the otherwise humdrum little hatchback included a striking pearlescent paintjob which flips from gold to pink as it drives by. Also a flamboyant gold Indian silk interior, fluorescent pink

highlights and delicate backlit illumination for the pink instruments which are viewed through a bespoke pink Connolly hide steering wheel with gold chromate detailing. Smashing.

And if that lot hasn't put you off, you might like to look out for one of the following limited editions in your copy of *Exchange & Mart*:

Car	Year	No. Built
Christian Audigier Lamborghini Murcielago	2008	5
Courreges Matra-Simca Bagheera	1974	650+
Dunhill Aston Martin DB7	2002	10
Gucci Cadillac Seville	1979	200
Jasper Conran Mazda MX-5	2000	500
Range Rover In Vogue	1981	700
Sisley Fiat Panda	1987	600
Versace Lamborghini Murcielago	2006	10

VIP – RTA – RIP: 10 CELEBS WHO CHECKED OUT EARLY

Eddie Cochran (1938–60)

With hits like 'C'mon Everybody' and 'Summertime Blues' – on which he sang and performed every part – Cochran had only one album to his credit when he died and was already the finest exponent of teenage rockabilly. Dead at twenty-one, his iconic status was ensured, especially when it was noted with macabre fascination that the Cochran single topping the UK charts at the time was 'Three Steps to Heaven'. Accompanied by his touring partner 'sweet Gene' Vincent – another American performer who was bigger in Britain than at home – he died in an accident on the road to London airport when the teenage driver of his Ford Consul minicab lost control. Vincent survived but inherited a limp as a result of injuries sustained.

James Dean (1931–55)

Dean's big break on Broadway came in *See the Jaguar* in 1952, but it was in a Porsche that he broke his neck after overcooking it in a new 550 Spyder bought three days previously. Its chassis number was memorable: 550-055 and he had George Barris, creator of the original Batmobile, paint the rear panel with the legend 'Little B*stard', before colliding with a black Ford sedan driven by one Donald Turnupseed. With Dean dead, the world's most famous car wreck was toured around exhibitions in a bid to discourage adolescents from driving dangerously and soon acquired its own legends as the 'car with a curse'. Initially it was fire damaged, then on two occasions it fell off its stand, first breaking a mechanic's legs then in 1959 injuring a teenage bystander. When its transporter was involved in an accident the driver was killed, the wreck itself disappeared from a goods yard, and in 1968 Dean's mechanic – injured in the crash but not fatally – was convicted of murdering his own wife.

Albert Camus (1913–60)

As much a man of action as a man of letters, Camus was a hero of the French Resistance, winner of the Nobel prize for literature and once played in goal for Algeria. The novelist, actor, playwright and journalist was also something of a philosopher, although he later argued and fell out with his friend Jean Paul Sartre. These days he's best remembered for an existentialist novel, *The Stranger* – 'the study of an absurd man in an absurd world' – but travelling with his publisher he was killed when the latter's Facel Vega whacked into a tree at an estimated 110mph.

T.E. Lawrence (1888–1935)

Turning his back on fame after the war and assuming the name John Ross then later T.E. Shaw – although many now believe this was merely a ruse to garner even more self-publicity – 'Lawrence of Arabia' sought solitude in rural Dorset. Obsessed with speed (and frequently economical with the truth: he once boasted he'd outrun a Bristol fighter plane while riding Boanerges, one of his six Brough Superior motorbikes) Lawrence fractured his skull and died after crashing another Brough at high speed outside the village of Moreton on Friday 13 May. A black saloon was mentioned at the inquest but never traced prompting rumours that the hero was still alive and the accident merely a cover for another Lawrence escapade.

Isadora Duncan (1878–1927)

The San Francisco-born dancer, creator and practitioner of a scandalous new style of dance was a controversial figure whom tragedy doggedly

pursued like a faithful hound. Interest in her private life was always high, particularly after her two young children were killed when the car in which they were travelling stalled and rolled backwards into the River Seine. She later married the Soviet poet laureate Sergei Esenin, who then killed himself leaving her a suicide note written in his own blood. Finally, on 14 September 1927, shortly after detailing the miseries of her life in an autobiography, she was accidentally strangled to death when her shawl became caught up in the rear wheel of a red Amilcar (not the Bugatti of legend) which she was considering buying.

Mike Hawthorn (1929–59)

Tall, blond and the first Briton to win the F1 World Championship, Ferrari's Mike Hawthorn was very much the Golden Boy of racing. (Such was his reputation that it even survived accusations that he was in part responsible for deaths of more than 80 spectators during the horrific 1955 Le Mans race.) After losing his team mates Mike Collins and Luigi Musso in 1958, Hawthorn quit racing but soon afterwards clipped a kerb in his hopped-up Jaguar Mark II. Nicknamed the Merc-Eater, he did it while overtaking fellow racing driver Rob Walker's gullwing Mercedes on the Guildford bypass at more than 100mph, spinning through 180 degrees and hitting a traffic island and a passing truck before shooting off the road. Dead, and not yet thirty, he was buried next to his father who'd been killed a few years earlier after being thrown from a Lancia Aurelia.

Princess Grace of Monaco (1928–82)

Beautiful, the daughter of a wealthy self-made Philadelphia Irish businessman, and one of the brightest talents at the American Academy of Dramatic Art, Grace Kelly enjoyed a brief but successful television and film career playing cool, elegant and detached beauties in films such as *High Noon* with Gary Cooper, *High Society*, and *To Catch a Thief* with Cary Grant. In 1956 she gave it all up to marry His Serene Highness Prince Rainier III of Monaco but her fairytale life ended suddenly after she had a fatal stroke at the wheel of her Rover P6.

Jackson Pollock (1912–56)

Born in Cody, Wyoming, Pollock was America's leading exponent of hurling pots of paint at great big canvases. Frequently room-size, his artworks became increasingly violent, confrontational and, like his own lifestyle, inexplicable to the viewer. (*Echo & Blue Poles*, for example, used no blue paint.) Then in 1956 his avowedly self-destructive bohemianism reached a peak when, depressed, drunk and drugged-up, he took his mistress and her girlfriend out for a spin in his 1950 Oldsmobile convertible and crashed into some trees on Long Island. The next day under a headline 'Still Life' the local newspaper carried a photograph of two cans of Rheingold beer, a hubcap and one of the artist's loafers.

Tara Browne (1945–66)

A racily decadent young aristocrat, one of the decade's grooviest new fashion designers and the perfect exponent of the fluid class structure of the Swinging Sixties, the Hon. Tara Browne, son of Lord Oranmore and Browne, perished in perfect sixties fashion behind the wheel of his trendy sky-blue Lotus Elan in Chelsea. He died after hitting a parked car, newspaper gossip columnists at the time observing that the twenty-one-year-old had been living at the Ritz Hotel and had dressed Lord Killearn's son-in-law in a 'striped frockcoat with velvet collar and cuffs.' Shortly after his death Browne was immortalised by the Beatles as the man who 'blew his mind out in a car' in *A Day in the Life*.

Marc Bolan (1947–77)

A mod and a model before discovering flower power and changing his name, Hackney-born Mark Feld attempted to form a five-piece electric band but, according to legend, was forced to scale it down to a two-piece acoustic outfit when most of the instruments were repossessed. The hippie-dippie philosophy of the resulting combo, Tyrannosaurus Rex, is best characterised by the title of their first album – 'My People Were Fair And Had Sky In Their Hair But Now They're Content To Wear Stars On Their Brows' – but catching the spirit of the moment they quickly switched to glam-rock and briefly hit the big time. At the start of a much heralded comeback, said to include his own TV series, Bolan was killed in a crash when his Mini hit a tree in south-west London.

OTHER DISTINCTIVE EXTINCTIONS

Eric Fernihough, the last Englishman to hold the Motorcycle World Speed Record, died on St George's Day 1938.

After crashing at Brooklands in 1913, Percy Lambert was buried at Brompton Cemetery in a coffin streamlined to match his car. Nearly a century later the *Sun* newspaper reported that a Bedfordshire teenager had been buried in a bespoke coffin shaped like a Ford Focus.

The first man to sink a productive oil well, the self-styled 'Colonel' Edwin L. Drake, nevertheless died penniless in Bethlehem, Pennsylvania.

The gravestone of racing driver Tazio Nuvolari (1892–1952) reads 'You will drive even faster on the highways of Heaven'.

Since the 1967 introduction of the breathalyser in the UK, car numbers have more than doubled but drink-drive fatalities fallen by more than half.

Motor industry giants Ettore Bugatti, Henry Ford, Louis Delage and GM founder Billy Durant all died in 1947.

As recently as April 2007 the press reported the case of a Tamil Nadu farmer who loved his old Morris so much that when he died his relatives decided to bury him in it.

A 1913 Talbot was the first car to cover 100 miles in one hour at Brooklands. Unfortunately, it later toppled over killing the driver.

William Crapo Durant founded the giant General Motors but died a relatively poor man after quitting the motor industry to work in supermarkets.

Hirschel E. Thornton Jr., a veteran of the Second World War, opened the world's first drive-in mortuary – in Atlanta, Georgia, – in which loved ones' caskets are conveniently tilted towards callers so that 'skilful drivers don't have to stop, and can just change right down and coast by.'

In 1970 the *Daily Telegraph* reported that the President of Toyota Cars had spent £168,000 building a 600sq ft shrine of 'blood red concrete' to commemorate the souls of all the people killed by the company's cars.

6

THE GOOD, THE BAD AND THE UGLY

CAR OF THE YEAR? SERIOUSLY?

Keen to defend their decisions the members of the Car of the Year jury claim their award is the most prestigious of the hundreds offered each year, and that their aim is simple – to find a 'single, decisive winner'. The victors tend to go along with that assessment, but many others refuse to, pointing out that the jury is no more than a self-selected group of hacks. More significantly, and not infrequently, the winners turn out to be also-rans while many evidently superior cars – the Ford Mustang, VW Golf, Audi 100 and Audi A2 to name but four – find themselves placed second, third or even not at all. Did anyone, anywhere, ever, *really* consider the Simca 1307 the best car in the world? Or the Renault 9? And hands up if you've even seen an Audi 50.

Year	First	Second	Third
1964	Rover 2000	Mercedes 600	Hillman Imp
1965	Austin 1800	Autobianchi Primula	Ford Mustang
1966	Renault 16	R-R Silver Shadow	Oldsmobile Toronado
1967	Fiat 124	BMW 1600	Jensen FF
1968	NSU Ro 80	Fiat 125	Simca 1100
1969	Peugeot 504	BMW 2500/2800	Alfa Romeo 1750
1970	Fiat 128	Autobianchi A112	Renault 12
1971	Citroën GS	Volkswagen K70	Citroën SM
1972	Fiat 127	Renault 15/17	Mercedes 350SL
1973	Audi 80	Renault 5	Alfa Romeo Alfetta
1974	Mercedes 450S	Fiat X1/9	Honda Civic
1975	Citroën CX	Volkswagen Golf	Audi 50
1976	Simca 1307–1308	BMW 3-series	Renault 30 TS
1977	Rover 3500	Audi 100	Ford Fiesta
1978	Porsche 928	BMW 7-series	Ford Granada
1979	Chrysler Horizon	Fiat Ritmo	Audi 80
1980	Lancia Delta	Opel Kadett	Peugeot 505

Year	First	Second	Third
1981	Ford Escort	Fiat Panda	Austin Metro
1982	Renault 9	Opel Ascona	Volkswagen Polo
1983	Audi 100	Ford Sierra	Volvo 760
1984	Fiat Uno	Peugeot 205	Volkswagen Golf
1985	Opel Kadett	Renault 25	Lancia Thema
1986	Ford Scorpio	Lancia Y10	Mercedes E-Class
1987	Opel Omega	Audi 80	BMW 7-series
1988	Peugeot 405	Citroën AX	Honda Prelude
1989	Fiat Tipo	Opel Vectra	Volkswagen Passat
1990	Citroën XM	Mercedes-Benz SL	Ford Fiesta
1991	Renault Clio	Nissan Primera	Opel Calibra
1992	Volkswagen Golf	Opel Astra	Citroën ZX
1993	Nissan Micra	Fiat Cinquecento	Renault Safrane
1994	Ford Mondeo	Citroën Xantia	Mercedes C-Class
1995	Fiat Punto	Volkswagen Polo	Opel Omega
1996	Fiat Bravo/Brava	Peugeot 406	Audi A4
1997	Renault Scénic	Ford Ka	Volkswagen Passat
1998	Alfa Romeo 156	Volkswagen Golf	Audi A6
1999	Ford Focus	Opel Astra	Peugeot 206
2000	Toyota Yaris	Fiat Multipla	Opel Zafira
2001	Alfa Romeo 147	Ford Mondeo	Toyota Prius
2002	Peugeot 307	Renault Laguna	Fiat Stilo
2003	Renault Mégane	Mazda 6	Citroën C3
2004	Fiat Panda	Mazda 3	Volkswagen Golf
2005	Toyota Prius	Citroën C4	Ford Focus
2006	Renault Clio	Volkswagen Passat	Alfa Romeo 159
2007	Ford S-Max	Opel/Vauxhall Corsa	Citroën C4 Picasso
2008	Fiat 500	Mazda2	Ford Mondeo
2009	Opel Insignia	Ford Fiesta	Volkswagen Golf

CAR OF THE YEAR:
MOST WINS BY MANUFACTURER

9	Fiat
6	Renault
5	Ford
3	Citroën
3	Opel/Vauxhall
3	Peugeot

2	Alfa Romeo
2	Audi
2	Chrysler/Simca
2	Rover
2	Toyota
1	Austin
1	Lancia
1	Mercedes-Benz
1	Nissan
1	NSU
1	Porsche
1	Volkswagen

NICE ONE, HENRY: TIN LIZZY SCOOPS CAR OF THE CENTURY

Somewhat less controversially, and to mark the end of the millennium, at the 1999 Frankfurt Show the results of a global poll to determine the Car of the Century were revealed. Drawn from a shortlist of 26 different models – cars selected by members of the public as well as by panel of so-called industry experts – the eventual winners are shown overleaf.

AC Cobra	1965–1967
Alfa Romeo Giulietta Sprint Coupé	1954–1968
Audi Quattro	1980–1991
Austin Seven	1922–1939
BMW 328	1936–1940
Bugatti Type 35	1926–1930
Chevrolet Corvette Sting Ray	1963–1967
Citroën Traction Avant	1934–1957
Citroën 2CV	1948–1990
Citroën DS19	1955–1975
Ferrari 250 GT SWB Berlinetta	1959–1962
Fiat 500 Topolino	1936–1948
Ford Model T	1908–1927
Ford Mustang	1964–1968
Jaguar XK120	1948–1954
Jaguar E-Type	1961–1975
Mercedes-Benz S/SS/SSK	1927–1932
Mercedes-Benz 300 SL 'Gullwing'	1954–1957
Mini	1959–2000

NSU Ro80	1967–1976
Porsche 911	1963 to date
Range Rover	1970 to date
Renault Espace	1984 to date
Rolls-Royce Silver Ghost	1907–1925
Volkswagen Beetle	1946–2003
Volkswagen Golf	1974 to date
Willys Jeep	1941–1945

… And the winners are …

1	Ford Model T	742 points
2	Mini	617 points
3	Citroën DS	567 points
4	Volkswagen Beetle	521 points
5	Porsche 911	303 points

THE CAR AS ART – MOMA

It took until 1951 for New York's prestigious Museum of Modern Art (MoMA) to properly acknowledge the machine that changed the world, since when a number of cars have been granted the honour of a plinth in the museum as exemplars of what sometime curator Arthur Drexler referred to as 'rolling sculpture'.

Audi Al2 Concept
Bentley 4.5 litre
Chrysler CCV Concept
Cisitalia 202
Cord 812
Fiat Multipla
Ford Ka
GM EV1
Honda Insight
Lincoln Continental
MCC Smart
Mercedes Benz SS
MG TC
Rover Mini Concept
Talbot Lago
Toyota Prius
Willys Jeep

THE CAR AS ART – BMW

In 1975 BMW took the art-car thing a stage further, when the racing
driver and auctioneer Hervé Poulain commissioned his friend American
artist Alexander Calder to do a special paintjob on a BMW 3.0 CSL.
Poulain later raced the car at Le Mans, coming nowhere as it happens,
but the idea caught on with miniature replicas being produced of several

future Art Cars while the originals went on display at leading galleries around Europe. To date the series comprises the following examples:

1975	Alexander Calder	3.0 CSL
1976	Frank Stella	3.0 CSL
1977	Roy Lichtenstein	320i Group 5
1979	Andy Warhol	M1 Group 4
1982	Ernest Fuchs	635 CSi
1986	Robert Rauschenberg	635 CSi
1989	Ken Done	M3 Group A
1989	Michael Nelson	M3
1990	Matazo Kayama	535i
1990	Cesar Manrique	730i
1991	Esther Mahlangu	525i
1991	A. R. Penck	Z1
1992	Sandro Chia	M3 GTR
1995	David Hockney	850 CSi
1999	Jenny Holzer	V12 LMR
2007	Olafur Eliasson	H2R
2009	Robin Rhode	Z4

THE EYE OF THE BEHOLDER

When America's *Automobile* magazine listed the 25 most beautiful cars ever – and included the Nissan 300ZX and 1966 Oldsmobile Toronado – it became clear that motoring journalists could no longer be trusted. Perhaps with this in mind, and for the cover story of its March 2009 issue, *Classic & Sports Car* decided to consult the experts.

The magazine polled 20 leading car stylists, past and present, asking them to describe what they considered to be the most beautiful cars of all time. To put their choices into some kind of perspective the designers were also asked to say which of their own designs – concept or production car – they were most proud of.

Designer	Most Proud Of	Most Admires
Giorgetto Giugiaro	Bugatti EB112	Citroën DS
Peter Stevens	McLaren F1	Citroën DS
Marcello Gandini	No interest in past work	Citroën DS
Tom Karen	Reliant Scimitar GTE	Cord 810/812
Gordon Murray	McLaren F1	Ferrari Dino 206S

Designer	Most Proud Of	Most Admires
John Heffernan	Aston Martin Vantage	Ferrari 250GT Lusso
Patrick Le Quement	Renault Twingo	Ferrari 250GT Lusso
Ian Callum	Jaguar XF	Ferrari 250GT SWB
Tom Tjaarda	De Tomaso Pantera	Ferrari 275 GTB
Leonardo Fioravanti	Ferrari Daytona	Ferrari 330 PS/4
Ken Okuyama	Maserati Quattroporte	Ferrari Dino 246GT
Steve Crijns	Lotus Evora	Ford GT40
Dennis Adams	Adams Roadster	Hispano-Suiza H6
Roy Axe	MG EX-E	Jaguar XK120
Martin Smith	Ford Fiesta	Lamborghini Countach
Julian Thomson	Jaguar R Coupé	Lamborghini Gallardo
Russell Carr	Lotus Evora	Lotus Elan +2
Oliver Winterbottom	Lotus Elite	Maserati Boomerang
Paolo Martin	Ferrari Dino	Alfa Romeo Canguro
Paul Bracq	BMW Turbo	Bugatti Type 41 Royale

CAR DESIGNER OF THE CENTURY

In 1999 the aforementioned Sr. Giugiaro was named 'Car Designer of the Century' after a poll of 132 journalists in 33 countries. Selecting him from the shortlist comprising those names shown overleaf, the panel highlighted a lifetime's achievement encompassing such landmarks as the Maserati Ghibli, Audi 80, Alfa Romeo Alfasud, Volkswagen Golf, Volkswagen Scirocco, Fiat Uno, Lotus Esprit, Lancia Delta … and the ill-fated DeLorean DMC-12.

Battista Farina	Too many Ferraris to count
Bill Mitchell	Chevrolet Corvette, Chevrolet Corvair
Bruno Sacco	Mercedes Benz S-Class
Ercole Spada	Aston Martin DB4 GTZ, Alfa Romeo TZ, Osca GT
Eric Gantt	Ford Taurus, Ford Sierra
Flaminio Bertoni	Citroën DS, Citroën 2CV, Citroën Ami
Giovanni Michelotti	Triumph Herald and TR4, Renault Alpine A110
Gordon Buehrig	Cord 810
Harley Earl	Cadillac LaSalle
Jack Telnack	Ford Mustang
Jan Wilsgaard	Volvo Amazon, Volvo 144, Volvo 240, Volvo 850
Jean Bugatti	Bugattis Type 57 Ventoux, Stelvio and Atalante
Leonardo Fioravanti	Ferrari Daytona, Ferrari Berlinetta Boxer
Marcello Gandini	Lamborghini Miura, Fiat X1/9, Lancia Stratos
Mario Revelli di Beaumont	Simca 1000, Fiat 6C 1500
Nuccio Bertone	BAT (Berlina Aerodinamica Technica) Alfa Romeos
Patrick le Quément	Renault Twingo, Renault Mégane Scénic
Pietro Frua	Fiat 1100 A Sport Barchetta, Maserati A6GS
Raymond Loewy	Hupmobile, Studebaker Avanti
Robert Opron	Citroën SM, Citroën GS, Citroën CX
Sixten Sason	Saab 93, Saab 99
Tom Gale	Dodge Viper, Chrysler Atlantic/Thunderbolt Concepts
Virgil Exner	1957 Chrysler 300, Dodge Custom Royal
Wayne Cherry	Vauxhall Equus, Pontiac Solstice, Cadillac Sixteen

IGNORAH AT YOUR PERIL: THE DREADFUL DOCKERS STRIKE

For much of the 1950s Daimler enthusiasts and gossip-columnists alike were agog at the antics of the boss and his wife, the flamboyant millionaire Sir Bernard Docker and his socially ambitious and highly acquisitive thrice-married wife Norah.

The once illustrious company was by this time far from secure, its sales badly damaged by post-war petrol rationing and an increase of purchase tax to 66.6 per cent dealing a near-fatal blow to an already traumatised

British luxury car market. Lady Docker's solution was to spend, spend, spend and – determined that the company could no longer depend on the royal family – plans were laid for a series of spectacularly extravagant show cars. Show cars to which, of course, she and her husband would have exclusive access.

1951 The Gold Car
In 1950 the company had had the most expensive car on show at Earls Court, a massive straight-eight DE-36 roadster nicknamed the Green Goddess and tipping the scales at £7,001. The following year Lady Docker's Gold Car was to knock that one into a cocked hat, however, a limousine embellished with an estimated 7,000 gold stars, and featuring throughout gold in place of chrome and an interior trimmed in golden camphor wood and gold brocade.

1952 Blue Clover
Topping this wouldn't be easy, but the next year she gave it a go, exhibiting a close-coupled two-door coupe, externally quite a lithe form but painted an absurdly feminine powder blue and pale grey at a time when most women still couldn't drive let alone afford to buy a car. If anything the interior was even worse, with matching lizard skins (dyed grey-blue to match) on the steering wheel, although even this was unable to conceal that beneath the glitz the car was a mechanical dinosaur.

1953 Silver Flash
Based on the old Conquest Century – its 3-litre, six-cylinder engine now almost twenty years old – the next car took its inspiration from

the BSA Golden Flash motorcycle (Sir Bernard was also the boss of BSA) but at the last minute this was resprayed silver when Lady Docker decided this went better than gold would with her garish black leather and red crocodile interior scheme.

1954 Stardust
After this the fourth car saw a return to the 'star' theme, the car finished in Royal Blue and covered in more miniature stars with the upholstery and trim made of silver silk brocatelle (the fabric especially made for the Dockers on hand-looms) with pale blue crocodile used for the door caps and cabinet work.

1955 Golden Zebra
Finally, Norah's last car looked to the longer DK400 limousine chassis, its ageing and mechanically unadventurous 4.6-litre straight-six propelling the vast two-door coupe finished in ivory white, embellished with gold – of course – and with zebra-skin upholstery. The whole ensemble reportedly cost the company £12,000, this at a time when a standard Daimler Conquest was so-named because at its introduction it sold for a whimsical if comparatively penny-pinching £1,066.

The following year the pair took the Golden Zebra across the water, to Monaco for the wedding of Prince Rainier to Grace Kelly – but the writing was on the wall. The public had had enough of such ostentation, and the Dockers' showmanship was beginning to go down very badly with the Daimler board. It didn't help matters when the Dockers were investigated for financial irregularities, having failed to declare the correct amount of money taken out of the country on the trip to Monaco. Nor when the company began to examine the extent of the couple's positively parliamentary 'business expenses'.

Her tongue perhaps loosened by too much pink champagne, Lady Docker went on the offensive, saying 'We bring glamour and happiness into drab lives. The working class loves everything I do.' – but it was to little avail and in late 1956 Sir Bernard was ousted from the Daimler board. Admitting she was miserable at the outcome the redoubtable Norah nevertheless insisted, 'It's not the loss of the gold cars that makes me feel like this. (And weren't they fun? They were like my children.) No, it's that lovely party I was planning for 25,000 of the company's workers for my 50th birthday. A tiptop affair – and now it's all off. How could they do this to [Sir Bernard] after seventeen years? Why, he's such a hard worker that he even had a direct line to the firm from our yacht *Shemara*.'

Alas the good ship *Shemara* also went in the end, eventually ending up in Suffolk after being bought by the reclusive Harry Hyams. The jewellery was sold too, and barred from Monaco the couple eventually retired to a bungalow in the Channel Islands. Lady Docker finally died in a Paddington hotel.

ALL DONE IN THE BEST POSSIBLE TASTE: IT WASN'T JUST THE DOCKERS...

America's 1950s fin-fad reached its peak with the Cadillac Fleetwood Sixty Special.

After crash-testing a Lamborghini Espada in 1973, the British importer had the remains silver-plated, called it art and mounted it on a plinth in his garden.

Henry Ford liked the Cotswolds so much he bought a cottage in Chedworth, dismantled it and had it shipped home and rebuilt in Michigan.

After breaking several world speed records, Bill Knight turned his streamlined 1957 Cooper upside down and used it as a garden pond.

The car which inspired Billie Holiday's 'Solid Gold Cadillac' had real leopardskin upholstery but in reality was only gold-plated.

The star of the 1947 Paris motor show, a special-bodied Bentley MkVI convertible, was upholstered with 1,250 Filipino frog skins.

CRAZY HORSES: THE 10 BIGGEST-EVER ENGINES

Obviously these days we're all keen to be as green as the next man but sometimes, clearly, there's just no substitute for cubic inches....

Biggest in a Ferrari: 7 Litres

For years European sports car makers snootily dismissed the Yanks' simple trusting faith in cubic inches, choosing to combat their crude 'lazy litres' with clever technology . . . at least until the Ford GT40 and McLaren's Chevrolet-engined M8 began to dominate at Le Mans and in Can-Am. Eventually even Enzo was stung into action, wheeling out the Ferrari 712 – 7 litres, 12 cylinders – in an attempt to silence the American upstarts once and for all. Unfortunately it failed, and the reds stepped back from sports car racing although the car itself still looks (and is) magnificent.

Biggest in a Land Speed Record Breaker: 73 Litres

These days it's all jets and rockets, but once upon a time they used cars to break the land speed records – if by cars you mean petrol engines driving wheels. Of these the largest was Captain George Eyston's *Thunderbolt* with 73 litres shared between two engines which between them developed a staggering 4,700 horsepower while consuming 5 gallons of fuel a minute. In August 1938 *Thunderbolt* hit 357.5mph but after the war the six-axled monster sadly perished in an arson attack although one of its Rolls-Royce R-Type aero engines survived to go on display at the Royal Air Force Museum, Hendon.

Biggest in a Rolls-Royce: 27 Litres

Everyone knows the Spitfire had a Rolls-Royce engine so eventually someone was bound to put a Spitfire engine into a Rolls – and that someone was Nick Harley. No stranger to expensive exotics – he'd previously bought a Grand Prix Mercedes and a Bugatti Royale – dropping a half-tonne Merlin into a 1938 Phantom II Continental must have seemed obvious. Fuel feed was a problem for the 1,000hp V12 – eventually NASCAR pumps did the trick at a rate of 100 gallons an hour – but now it's complete the towering torque means there's no need ever to shift out of top.

Biggest in a Circuit Racer: 24 Litres

After Captain Eyston's triumph it fell to his fellow Englishman John Cobb to lift the record over the magic 400mph mark – but not before he had made his name driving the magnificent 24-litre, W12-engined Napier-Railton. At Brooklands in 1935 it smashed (and still holds) the outright lap record at 143.44mph as well as posting the highest speed ever recorded at the famous Surrey circuit: a whisker under 152mph. More than twenty years later, the beast was still earning its keep – as a mobile test-bed for military parachutes.

Biggest in a Pimpmobile: 8.2 Litres

At a time when the Corvette was pegged at 350 cubic inches, the record for America's largest engine went to the 1970 Cadillac Eldorado with no fewer than 495 or something over 8 litres. A great slab-sided beast – fabulously redolent of the likes of *Shaft* and *Cannon* – its 400hp V8 seemed unbeatable at the time, and indeed GM didn't even bother trying, instead opting for a mere 7.7 litres when it came up for renewal in 1977. A favourite drive in a host of 'blaxploitation' movies, one also made it into 007's 1973 offering *Live and Let Die.*

Biggest in an Offroader: 7.2 Litres

In terms of capacity even the authentic, Desert Storm-issue Humvee takes a back seat to the Rambo Lambo, Italy's ill-fated foray off-road. Based on the company's 1977 Cheetah prototype – unfortunately written off by the US military during testing – at first it used a Chrysler V8 but eventually traded up to a 7.2-litre V12 originally intended for Class One offshore powerboats. A few were acquired by expanding oil-rich armies in Saudi Arabia and Libya but most were snapped up by sheikhs who found the car's bespoke Pirelli Scorpion tyres just the thing for hawking in the dunes.

Biggest in a Limousine: 12.7 Litres

Twenty-one feet long and with a fourteen-foot wheelbase, the Bugatti Type 41 – invariably known as the Royale – was the right car at the wrong time, or maybe just the wrong car altogether. Launched in 1929 just as a worldwide recession began to bite, it found no takers at all among its target audience – Europe's ruling families – and after just six examples had been built for sale a number of its straight-eight engines were redeployed pulling railway trains. One later sold at auction for a record-breaking £5.5 million, but not before Mrs Bugatti had disposed of hers by swapping it for a couple of refrigerators.

Biggest in a Dragster: 28.3 Litres

The pioneering drag-racer and serial land-speed record holder (see p. 77) Art Arfons built a series of so-called Green Monsters using war-surplus aero engines. Initially these were piston-driven, although in common with his rivals he eventually switched to jet power. In 1958, however, one of the former sporting an Allison V12 set a new A/Dragster benchmark when the 1,710-cubic inch unit enabled him to max out at 156.24mph. In qualifying he had reached 161.67mph, but for technical reasons this did not count towards the record. Three years later a similar engine took him to 313.78mph before lunching its clutch.

Biggest in a Smart: 5.67 Litres

The brainchild, if that's the word, of rally driver Stefan Attart the Smart Forfun2 mated the little Smart body to some monster Unimog 406 underpinnings including the latter's six-cylinder OM 352 diesel engine. Producing 84bhp – making it by far the puniest car here, despite having twice the punch of the original – it nevertheless turns heads wherever it goes thanks to its mammoth 65cm ground clearance, huge wheels and 3.7-metre height.

Biggest in a Concept Car: 13.6 Litres

In the 1930s Cadillac created the luxurious V16 and seventy years later revisited the idea with the 1,000hp/1,000lb per foot Cadillac Sixteen Concept. This time it came with a 'green' twist though, something called Displacement on Demand technology shutting down half the cylinders to reduce emissions then automatically reactivating them when the driver's right foot decides they're needed. Unfortunately its chances of going into production were never rated higher than slim.

A BASKET OF LEMONS:
DAFT IDEAS AND DEAD ENDS

University of California Professor George Akerlof was the first to describe a car as a lemon – introducing the expression in a 1970s economics paper headed *The Market for Lemons: Quality Uncertainty And Market Mechanisms*

– but the industry was way ahead of him having by then been making and selling duff designs for decades. Incidentally, the opposite was a known as a cherry, Prof. Akerlof presumably having chosen this term before driving Datsun's 100A Cherry which was launched the same year.

1934 Voisin 12

The legendary Gabriel Voisin was something of an eccentric and at the age of 93 told an enthusiast, 'don't worry about my old cars. At your age you should be out chasing women.' Aside from tartan body panels, his most extraordinary move was to build a straight-twelve, effectively two in-line sixes arranged in a row, the idea being to bring the centre of gravity closer to the centre of the car. Unfortunately it brought the engine closer to the occupants, the engine being so long that it penetrated deep into the passenger compartment bringing with it all the noise, heat and vibration of a massive power plant. Just three were built before common sense intervened.

1934 Chrysler Airflow

Chrysler launched its Airflow sedan after deciding that most cars at the time were aerodynamically more efficient when travelling in reverse. They might have been right, but the public wasn't yet ready for the solution: a car which conspired to be at once flowing and awkward, with huge, sad-looking headlamps and a long, protruding bug-like snout. In fact the car was so ugly – nearly as ugly as France's Rosengart Supertraction which many likened to a dead fish – that before caving in and scrapping it altogether Chrysler took the unprecedented step of

offering a replacement nose which owners could retro-fit should they so choose to do.

1964 Vanden Plas Princess R

Vanden Plas, the prestige, coachbuilding end of British Leyland's precursor BMC, stuck a 4-litre, six-cylinder Rolls-Royce B60 engine into an Austin A110 four-door saloon and called it the Princess R. The first and so far last time Rolls-Royce has ever supplied an engine to a rival carmaker, the mistake perhaps – given that looking the part has always been an important element of Rolls-Royce ownership – was that they didn't do it the other way round. A car which looked like a Roller but was priced liked an ordinary Austin would have appealed to cheese-paring niggards everywhere – which this one certainly never did.

1967 NSU Ro80

Elegant but doomed, NSU's flirtation with Dr Felix Wankel's revolutionary engine technology reached its apotheosis with this one. Wankel insisted conventional pistons were inefficient – although critics could have told him that at least they worked properly, which was more than could be said for his rotary alternative. Unfortunately rotor-tip seal failure and a huge thirst for oil meant his engines often had to be replaced every 10,000 miles or so making a car which was expensive to buy even more so just to keep on the road. When VW-Audi took over in 1969 there was just one stipulation: no more Wankels. Today they're much sought after, however, many having had a much improved Mazda engine substituted for the original.

1975 AMC Pacer

If you've never heard of AMC, here's why. Together with its sister car the Gremlin – can you believe anyone would name a car such a thing? – this strangely short, gumdrop-shaped blob was a 1970s attempt at an American economy car. Unfortunately a decision to equip it with a 5.0-litre V8 meant the most owners could expect was around 14–15mpg. Also rust was a major problem from the start while the admirable practicality of its rear hatchback was wholly undermined by its especially-easy-to-pick lock.

1975 Triumph TR7

BL's wedge was supposed to be the shape of the future, but instead it made most enthusiasts hanker after the clean, no-nonsense lines of its chunky TR6 predecessor. After seeing the new Triumph TR7 in profile at an auto show, Italdesign's Giorgetto Giugiaro is said to have whispered to a colleague, 'just don't tell me they've done the same to the other side too'. (A bit like the spy photographer who didn't bother snapping an early prototype of the Jaguar XJS as he couldn't believe they would ever put anything that ugly into production.)

THE BUICK-ROVER V8: SIMPLY THE BEST?

Almost certainly not, but it's certainly among the longest-lived of internal combustion engines and one of the most versatile too. Having grown over the years from 3.5 litres to a thumping 5, it's powered everything from saloons and off-roaders through sports cars to pukka military ATVs.

At launch it was the lightest mass-production V8 in the world, fitted as standard to the 1961 Buick Special along with the Oldsmobile F-85, Cutlass and Jetfire models and Pontiac's Tempest and LeMans. It also ran to good effect in a number of competition cars, forming the basis of Brabham's Repco V8 which won the 1966 and 1967 Formula 1 World Championships.

Unfortunately the relatively high cost of the aluminum engine quickly led to its cancellation by the US auto industry after the 1963 model year, and in 1965 the tooling was sold for a song to Rover. That company stuck with it in one form or another for more than three decades with GM at one point attempting to buy it back and then declining Rover's offer to sell them engines when the British company refused to let it go home. Since then it has powered the following:

3.5 Litres

1967	Rover P5
1968	Lotus Type 47D
1968	Morgan Plus 8
1968	Rover P6B
1970	Land Rover Range Rover
1973	MGB GT V8
1975	Land Rover 101 Forward Control
1976	Argyll
1976	Rover SD1
1978	Land Rover Series III 'Stage One'
1979	Triumph TR8
1980	TVR 350i
1983	Land Rover 90/110/Defender
1985	Sherpa 400 Van

1986   Sisu NA-140 BT ATV (weird Finnish Army snowmobile)
1989   Land Rover Discovery
1996   LDV Convoy Van

3.9 Litres
1984   Marcos Spider 3.9 SE
1984   TVR 390 SE
1986   TVR S
1986   Sisu NA-140 BT ATV
1989   Land Rover Range Rover
1991   Westfield SEight
1991   Ginetta G33
1991   Pegaso Z103
1992   MG RV8
1992   TVR Griffith
1992   TVR Chimaera
1994   Land Rover Defender
1995   Land Rover Range Rover SE

4.2 Litres
1986   TVR 420 SEAC
1992   Land Rover Range Rover

4.3 Litres
1992   TVR Griffith
1993   TVR Chimaera
1993   Westfield SEight

4.4 Litres

1973   Leyland P76
1995   Land Rover Range Rover HSE
1996   TVR Chimaera
2003   Land Rover Discovery

5.0 Litres

1992   TVR Chimaera
1992   TVR Griffith
1994   Marcos LM500
2002   Bowler Wildcat

FINALLY …

No-one's quite sure why, but in 2004 Tesco questioned 4,500 women drivers about their motoring preferences – in particular trying to ascertain which cars they felt were sexiest for men to drive, and which the least sexy. Few surprises, to be honest, but the results are shown below:

Top 10

1.   Aston Martin
2.   Porsche
3.   Lotus
4.   Mercedes-Benz
5.   BMW
6.   Jaguar
7.   Audi
8.   Range Rover
9.   Jeep
10.   Ferrari

Bottom 10

1.   Citroën 2CV
2.   Reliant Robin
3.   Skoda
4.   Lada
5.   Trabant
6.   Rover
7.   Lexus
8.   Ford Mondeo
9.   Daewoo
10.   Hyundai

On a related note a US survey once revealed that some 65 per cent of American adults would sooner forego sex than give up their cars for a day, while an astonishing 86 per cent of readers survey by *Men's Journal* admitted they would sooner drive a new Range Rover than date Claudia Schiffer.

MEN BEHAVING BADLY

HARDLY HERTZ AT ALL: FIVE FAVOURITE MANOEUVRES IN A RENTAL CAR

Front-wheel, rear-wheel or four-wheel drive – the handling debate starts the moment you pass your test. Enthusiasts can't resist rear wheel-drive and the chance to enjoy tyre-smoking starts, wild cornering on opposite lock, lurid tail slides and the rush of a four-wheel skid as they effortlessly drift through the apex of blind bend. By contrast, Mr and Mrs Well-Adjusted prefer the inherent stability of front-wheelers like the Austin Allegro and Nissan Micra, cars whose foolproof understeer prevents even hardened petrolheads indulging in anything more dangerous than the sound of Perry Como on Cosyslippers FM as they tootle down to Tesco's. And of course off-roaders prefer 4WD for its genuine go-anywhere ability. . .

. . . But they're all wrong. As P. J. O'Rourke long ago pointed out, the best handling car is someone-else's. On or off road, you can drive a rental car anywhere and punt it as fast as you like into the corners in any gear

you fancy. You can even park it – oops, sorry – without paying attention, but preferably only after trying your hand at these classic manoeuvres.

Handbrake Turn

A firm favourite, your basic boys-behaving-badly manoeuvre, and best of all you don't even need all that much power to play. Just crank up your speed in a straight line and pull the wheel hard over while yanking the handbrake up as quick as you can. With practice you should be able to spin through at least 180 degrees and drive off again without stalling.

J-Turn

A sort of reverse handbrake turn, only without the handbrake, this one's pure *Starsky & Hutch*. VIP chauffeurs learn it as an anti-kidnap manoeuvre but for the rest of us it's the ideal way to express dissatisfaction when you're stuck at the end of a slow-moving queue of traffic. Select reverse gear (it's not your car, of course, so you don't have to wait until you've coasted to a halt to do this) accelerate backwards as hard as you can before grasping the bottom of the wheel and pulling it right over. Get it right and the nose will swing through a semicircle, aiming the car in the opposite direction at which point you shove it into first gear, floor the accelerator and go for it.

Side-Stepping

For a fast getaway there's still nothing to beat dumping the clutch at maximum revs and fish-tailing down the strip. Trouble is, most of the time you just can't get your size tens off quick enough to catch it at the right time – that magic moment between the valves popping and actually bursting through the bonnet. Try holding the corner of the clutch pedal down with the very edge of your shoe. That way, the split second before the rev-limiter cuts in you can side-step it slightly so the pedal pops up, the clutch bites hard and off you go.

Standing Smokers

The same but standing still, this is harder to master than side-stepping and requires a little finesse. You don't get unlimited practice time either because if you don't manage to make the wheels spin you'll end up with a burned out clutch instead.

Doughnuts

We can do doughnuts too, though setting one up in a car is not easy, more a question of finely balanced steering and power-delivery than brute force. It's essential you forgo your mum's Fiesta for this one and instead grab something reasonably powerful and rear-wheel drive. Next you'll need to establish and maintain a constant-velocity oversteer environment in which the driven wheels are empowered to prescribe cyclical but unequal orbits around the stationary passive axle. Or to put it another way, get the tail out and keep it there. You'll find the car slides more easily on a broken or dusty surface, then just juggle your speed and steering until you eventually get it to spin round its nose.

LAZY LITRES: 10 FAST US-EURO HYBRIDS

Essentially a 1960s phenomenon – although much like recreational drug-taking it's a fashion which has outlasted the decade which spawned it – the success of the AC Cobra paved the way for a rash of sports cars whose creators sought to satisfy the need for speed by producing cars in which high-end European styling was paired with cheap, reliable and relatively unstressed power from huge, mass-produced V8s. Did someone say cheap? He meant only compared to a complex, sophisticated, multi-valve, multi-cam Italian V12.

1954 Facel Vega
Building everything from kitchen units to a bespoke Bentley body shell before going into business for himself, Jean Daninos tweaked the Bentley design, stuck in a 4.5-litre DeSoto Firedome V8 and called the result the Vega. Allied to his company name – short for Forges et Ateliers de Construction d'Eure et de Loire – it sold well despite being almost

twice the price of a range-topping Citroën DS and having a tin dash painted with a feather to look like wood. With the demise of Delage, Delahaye and Talbot-Lago making it France's only luxury manufacturer, a list of celebrity and royal owners must have helped, including the Shah of Iran and Morocco's King Hassan II.

1962 Shelby-AC Cobra

If imitation is the sincerest form of flattery, then this one's been flattered almost to death with literally hundreds of fakes out there for every genuine factory-built car. The Cobra's origins lie with the elegant but understated AC Ace, a little roadster which, fitted with a succession of Bristol and later Ken Rudd-tuned Ford Zephyr engines, proved competitive. Runner-up in the 2.0-litre class at Le Mans in 1957, it went on to win America's SCCA series – in Classes E, D and C – against the likes of the Porsche Carrera and Mercedes-Benz 300SL.

It was while watching the car scoop the 1961 championship that chicken farmer Carroll Shelby spotted the car's real potential, something he demonstrated by plonking a 4,260cc Ford V8 into an engineless car he had flown to California to prove his point. Having earlier failed to convince Aston Martin, Jensen and Maserati of the value of such a trans-Atlantic tie-up, even he admitted that his 7.0-litre variant would 'kill you in a second.' In the right hands though the cars were spectacular, and in 1967 the coupé version Shelby named the Daytona overhauled Ferrari to win the international GT Championship.

1963 TVR Griffith 200

Following fast and hard on the Cobra's heels, and with its Ford of America 289 cube V8 making it very much the ancestor of more recent TVRs, the Griffith 200 stuck a big engine into a small, stubby body. The name referred to its claimed output, although in reality this varied widely from about 190 to 270 thus presenting something of a challenge to the rear axle which was a standard BMC unit. Maximum speed was around 140mph, although with the car's balance badly upset by the much heavier nose it must have been quite a handful.

1964 Ford GT40

Shelby wasn't the only one who wanted to take the fight to Ferrari, and in 1964 – already active in drag, stock, track and international sports prototype racing – Ford decided to meet the Italians head on at Le Mans. Their weapon of choice was the GT40, famously named after its 40in height and based on Eric Broadley's little 1963 Lola GT. A 4.2-litre transplant failed to do the job – the first year out it won absolutely nothing

– and a 4.7 secured just one win the following year. For 1966 they upped the stakes considerably – to 7.0 litres – and promptly swept the board.

Coming first, second and third at both Daytona and Le Mans, the cars also took a 1-2 at Sebring just to show the whole thing hadn't been a fluke. Since then replicas have proliferated and with only 107 genuine cars ever completed – some detuned for the road, although owners often tune them back up again – it can be hard to tell what's genuine and what's not. (Not least, one might add, because in 2003 Ford produced its own homage in the form of the quite magnificent supercharged 5.4-litre Ford GT.)

1964 Sunbeam Tiger
Never enjoying quite the kudos of the Cobra, nor indeed its track record, the Tiger nevertheless shares many parallels with that one, Sunbeam boss Lord Rootes having recognised that, like the Ace, his Alpine looked the part but was dramatically underpowered. He too sought a solution in the US, his initial order for 4,000 V8s being the largest Ford had ever received from an outside firm. The 4.2 litre always did better in America than at home, and the later 4.7 was never officially offered here although seventeen somehow made it over with half a dozen being ordered by the fuzz.

1965 Iso Grifo
Initially a motorcycle maker before branching out into bubble cars – the iconic Isetta was made under licence in Germany, Italy, Spain, France and Brazil – in 1955 Iso sold the bubbles business to BMW and set its sights on the supercar segment. First up was the unfortunately named Rivolta – Bertone body, 5.4-litre Chevrolet V8 – quickly followed by the shorter and more stylish Grifo which could be ordered with a choice of a 300, 365 or 400bhp engine. The last-named employed a hefty 7.0-litre capable of 177mph, but the company was hit hard by the 1973 oil crisis and folded not long afterwards.

1965 Bizzarrini 5300 GT Strada
Initially kept busy by his rivals – formerly working for Alfa and Ferrari, Giotto Bizzarrini also designed stuff for Lamborghini and for Iso's Renzo Rivolta – he eventually got to design his own car using the aforementioned Grifo A3C as a base. Essentially a lightweight version of this, and employing a similar 5.4-litre Chevy mill, it was conceived as a dual-purpose road/race machine but sold in only tiny numbers even compared to the rare Iso. Later an attempt was made to create a smaller, economy model called the Europa, but with its 1.9-litre Opel engine it aroused little serious interest.

1966 Jensen Interceptor

If flared trousers were cars they'd look like this one, Jensen's outrageous, glass-backed sixties supercar somehow surviving through to 1976 despite an appetite for fuel which looked more appropriate for a factory than for a mere four-seater. Part of the problem was the 6.3-litre Chrysler V8, but the decision to go with four-wheel drive for the range-topping FF couldn't have helped either. That said it wasn't the OPEC oil shock which did for Jensen in the end, but rather a long-running saga of 1970s-style wrangles between the bosses and the workers.

1967 De Tomaso Mangusta

Naming his car 'Mongoose' because it ate Cobras – actually it never did – Alejandro de Tomaso was an Argentinian living in Italy. After building half a dozen F1 cars, and a Ford Cortina-powered road car called the Vallelunga, he led a buyout at Ghia and set the famous coachbuilder to work styling his own striking two-seater. Designed around a mid-placed 4.7-litre Ford V8 and a five-speed ZF transaxle, for a company with little heritage it did well selling around 400 over a four year period. Unfortunately it was expensive to build, and the performance and handling never quite lived up to its gorgeous looks.

1970 Monteverdi High Speed 375L

Sometime mechanic, racer and race-car manufacturer, Peter Monteverdi was also a successful car dealer in his native Switzerland. Eventually switching from single-seaters to luxury GTs, his distinctive designs utilised a variety of mammoth Chrysler V8s – up to 7.2 litres – and appeared in both two- and four-door guises with both long- and short-wheelbases. As an even more exclusive rival to the likes of the Jensen Interceptor, the name came from the engine's reputed output: 375bhp

10 PLACES WHERE YOU MIGHT
GET AWAY WITH IT
(AND ONE WHERE YOU PROBABLY WON'T)

Sweeping curves, broad open bends gently rising and falling as they follow the scenery, and not a truck or tractor in sight – remember the days when you could put your foot down on your favourite road and get away with it? When you might be lucky enough to meet a rozzer who actually liked cars, or one who couldn't be bothered to pull out his pad so close to going home time? But the Gatso never knocks off. One flash – two actually, seven-tenths of a second apart – and you're nicked and the first you know of it is when the summons arrives in the post.

In fact, until recently the boys in blue were never that bothered about speeding, providing you didn't take the mickey. But now, using a formidable hi-tech battery of cameras, Vascar, Muniquip, helicopter-mounted video and anything else he can find in the toy box, Mr Plod is set to take the fun out of motoring forever. Radar scanners and jammers aren't legal and don't work – you didn't really think a Chinese-made box of tricks costing £50 would beat a £30 grand camera did you? – so the game's up. Unless, that is, you're prepared to travel.

Bonneville Bombers
Since 1949 hot-rodders have flocked to Utah's famous blinding white salt flats with their promise of endless space, perfect weather conditions and, at 4,000ft above sea-level, the added bonus of reduced aerodynamic drag. With the right equipment 300mph is possible – there's a club for those who make it – and even if you lose it at 200mph the cars generally spin crazily but lazily across the salt rather than rolling you into oblivion. Bonny's official Speed Week takes place in August, and the nearest emergency hospital is at Tooele, 110 miles away .

Autobahn-Storming
In 1963 an AC Cobra reportedly hit 196mph on the M1 and shortly afterwards parliament moved to introduce the 70mph national speed limit. In Germany they didn't bother and today it's still legal to go for it on some stretches although much of the network now has a 130kph (81mph) 'advisory' limit with the *polizei* coming down heavily on anyone they feel is driving dangerously. Good lane discipline, much better than

in Britain, means accidents are rare but when they happen they happen big, and many Germans instead like to exercise their automotive muscle at the Nürburgring, a 14-mile closed loop they can thrash round for just £8 a pop.

Montana

It used to be Nevada where you went 'racing for pinks' – *American Graffiti*-style stand-offs, the prize being the pink ownership documents of your opponent's car – but eventually the state fell in line with the rest of America and its ridiculous 55mph top. A few years later Montana loosened up, proposing a 'no-limit' limit or rather no-stated-limit during daylight hours. Instead drivers are expected to drive at a speed which is 'reasonable and prudent' although precisely what the police consider prudent for an empty stretch of two-lane blacktop running dead straight for 10 miles across the prairies with nothing and no-one in sight varies from court to court.

Mirage Jet

Each summer the lakes at Muroc and El Mirage in the hostile Mojave Desert dry out leaving a flat alkaline bed as smooth as a pool table which bakes as hard as glass in the Southern Californian sun. El Mirage is actually government land but no-one seems to mind and with a broad track down the middle a mile and a half long it's just made for the job. In theory you can turn up in anything – not long ago an old Datsun did 169mph – but the real aficionados bring their own, weird high-octane machines often homemade using cut-and-shut Second World War aircraft droptanks favoured for their superb aerodynamics.

T-T-Terrific

Strange place, the Isle of Man, strict on some things – at one time corporal punishment in schools, for example – but incredibly lax on others, like speeding which they simply never got around to banning in the first place. The TT race, an event so fast and deadly that if it were proposed tomorrow it would be scrapped immediately, has been run on the mountain roads since the glory days when Britain outlawed racing on public roads and enthusiasts took their machines – bikes and cars – over to the island. On 'Mad Sunday' bikers traditionally go completely barmy (and some come home in a box) but for the rest of the year the mountain roads offer thrill-a-minute motoring for anyone renting a car from Ronaldsway Airport.

United Europe

At least until the EU gets its act together (and it will) to harmonise driving licences and introduce a system of pan-European endorsements and driving bans, it is still possible to nip across to the Continent for a bit of tail-up-nose-down naughty-naughty. They already do it to us, and more than a few Euro-bikers have nipped under the Channel, completed a few 130mph laps of the M25, and then scarpered back down the Tunnel before Kent's cops have cottoned on. High risk but big thrills providing you avoid those countries like France and Switzerland where fines are levied on-the-spot and can be very heavy.

'Ere, That's Sandy

In the 1920s Sir Malcolm Campbell, the first man to drive at 150mph, did it on Pendine Sands in Carmarthen Bay. A few years later racing driver Parry Thomas was buried there after his 27-litre special 'Babs' snapped a drivechain at 170mph and cut off his head. These days, if you don't mind having to dodge the donkeys and the deckchairs, the huge expanse of slightly damp and oh-so-flat sand that makes it Britain's Bonneville still provides a perfect place in which to let rip. But be warned: if Carmarthen County Council don't catch you at it, the salt corrosion will.

Haha Baja

Wider, smoother, longer, straighter and far, far emptier than your average American Interstate, Mexico's Highway One cuts through Ensenada which perhaps explains the local law enforcement authority's relaxed attitude to high-speed four-wheelers. Ensenada is home to America's answer to the Paris-Dakar, the Baja 500, and apparently there is a speed limit on Highway One but I couldn't see it nor could anyone tell me what it was.

Outback

Big and empty, very empty, the Australian hinterland's somewhere where speed limits are an irrelevance providing you remember to hit the brakes when you reach the city limits 2,000 miles down the road. Here you don't bother watching out for the police when you're tanking along, you watch out for the wildlife: hit a kangaroo at 110 and when the dust settles he won't be in any worse shape than you are. Also the roadtrains, those truck-trailer combos which make the average artic look as weenie as a panel van and which thunder coast-to-coast stopping for nothing and no-one. And that includes you.

Back to the Tracks

Most circuits organise the occasional track day where enthusiasts can let rip. As well as racing schools with their own fleets of single-seaters, these include 'run what you brung' events where you use your own cars. Contact the following circuits for days and dates, or contact Peter Gethin Driving Courses if you fancy having a former F1 driver teach you how to do it properly. Silverstone (01327 857413), Brands Hatch (01474 872331), Goodwood (01243 789660), Castle Combe (01249 782929), Donington Park, (01332 810048).

Helsinki

Probably worth avoiding Finland, however. In 2002 A director of the Finnish telecommunications giant Nokia appealed against what is believed to be the most expensive speeding ticket ever handed out After police said his Harley Davidson was doing 47mph in a 31mph zone, Anssi Vanjoki, 44, was fined 116,000 euros (£102,000) because the law in Finland allows fines to take an offender's annual income into account.

REDS ON YER: COOL COMMUNIST CARS

Maybe now the oil's running out what the speed-freaks really need is a new, altogether different definition of cool. Something other than that winning combination of cc, bhp, and mph. Something slow and rubbish and ugly, perhaps; in other words something Russian. Typically they're just ripped-off Western designs, tackily embellished with a uniquely

awful brand of totalitarian styling concealing lamentable build-quality and laughable, Stone Age engineering. Even so, a few of the cars built on the wrong side of the Iron Curtain have acquired something approaching cult status since the Berlin Wall was torn down, enabling a few handfuls of semi-roadworthy examples to putt-putter into the West.

Lada Niva
Simple, basic and authentically tractor-tough, the 1977 Niva was the first non-Fiat design to be built by Russia's AvtoVAZ factory and quickly proved popular thanks to its combination of durability and full-time four-wheel-drive. Selling as far away as Australia, it's still built under licence in Uruguay (where it sells as under the unlikely name of the Bognor Diva) while the wildest was almost certainly the version rebuilt by ex-police sergeant Dave McVay which at its peak was rumoured to produce around 170bhp.

Moskvitch 2141
A crude copy of a French Simca 1307 – and the first front-wheel-drive design from Moskovskji Zavod Maloitrashnyh Avtomobiley – the car was built on an old Opel production line which had been 'liberated' by the Red Army in 1945 before being shipped back to the Soviet Union and reassembled in Moscow. Inevitably at some point in its history the factory was renamed after Lenin, while the car itself took its name from the Russian for Muscovite, i.e. a resident of that city. Production began in 1986, peaking at 250,000 a year before collapsing to fewer than 3,000 a decade later.

Skoda 1100 OHC Spider
While the jokes have finally stopped, many car buffs still need reminding that Skodas weren't always cheap and nasty. It's true that the company was the only carmaker to have its factories bombed by both sides during the Second World War. And of course Skoda design and build quality were highly questionable (to say the least) during the Communist era. But Skoda was actually rather grand in the old days, building the Skoda Hispano-Suiza in the mid-1920s as well as creating its own elegant, Bugatti-like sports coupé called the Monte Carlo.

Under state control, however, all of that kind of thing stopped as production shifted to simple, no-nonsense designs like the 990 and 110 series. But there was the odd exception, of which this was the best: the 1957 1100 OHC with a relatively advanced tubular spaceframe chassis and a top speed of 120mph. For both political and economic reasons it was denied the chance to run at Le Mans – the car would have come nowhere, which was obviously never going to be acceptable – but it looked the part and managed an impressive 1-2 at a Communists-only race in Leningrad.

Tatra T603
Genuinely innovative, and from a company which in Hans Ledwinka had a truly pioneering chap at the helm, Tatra fell into Nazi hands in 1938 and then under Communist control when Ledwinka was found guilty of collaboration and gaoled for six years. In 1951 he fled to Austria but the company stayed close to Ledwinka's ideal, producing impressively aerodynamic, highly idiosyncratic designs using rear-mounted, air-cooled engines. Of these the 1955 T603 is the best known and most iconic, although sales were restricted to Party officials and friendly, left-leaning heads of state.

Trabant
Available as a saloon, an estate and even what passed for a limousine on the wrong side of the Berlin Wall, the 'Trabi' shot to fame when droves of the smoky little things crossed into the West following the long overdue collapse of Communism. A product of the Saxony-based VEB Sachsenring Automobilwerke Zwickau, its combination of laughably poor performance and shockingly bad emissions somehow won the affection of trendy Westerners indulging in a bit of 'Ostalgia'. An attempt was made to update it by replacing the 26hp two-stroke with a modern 1.0-litre VW Polo engine but perhaps all you needed to know about that one was that even then the company's PR director still preferred to come to work on a bicycle.

Velorex
In these greener times we've grown used to the idea of recycled, lightweight and even organic materials being used in cars but the Czech brothers Frantisek and Mojmir Stransky were already there in 1950. Seeking to avoid the high cost of steel by covering the tube frames of their 250cc three-wheelers with a woven material similar to leatherette, the brothers had started out designing simple cyclecars for wartime amputees. Unfortunately the government soon seized control and converted the factory into a workers' co-op.

Barkas B-1000
A sort of Commie Commer van, the B-1000 was built at the old Framo lorry works in Chemnitz which found itself in the Soviet-occupied zone when Germany was sliced up in 1945. With East Germany established as a separate state a few years later, and Chemnitz predictably renamed

Karl-Marx-Stadt, the factory became 'VEB Barkaswerke' and started turning out various small but flexible commercial vehicles. Produced from 1961 until 1990, the Barkas ran a modified, two-stroke 992cc Wartburg engine, but could still manage 50mph when fully loaded.

Volga GAZ-24

The Volga (pronounced Volha, after the river) served time as a taxi but more than anything was the preserve of Party apparatchiks who, while not without influence, found themselves too far down the pecking order to qualify for a ZIS or ZIL. From 1968 to 1985 it was built at the Gorky Automobile Plant, and early cars had the luxury of two wing mirrors where one was the Soviet norm. With a 2,445cc in-line four, performance was respectable rather than remarkable, but it was roomy and robust and having been designed for Russian roads and the Siberian climate, cars with 1,000,000 kilometres on the clock were by no means rare.

Wartburg 353

The original Wartburg was an 1895 copy of the French Decauville Voiturelle named after a local castle, and in 1955 the name was revived for a new series of three-cylinder cars built at Eisenach in East Germany. The 353 arrived in 1966, and being based on the Polish-built Warszawa 210 was available as a saloon or an estate known as the Kombi. Handsomely undercutting its GM and Ford rivals, as the Wartburg Knight it sold reasonably well in the UK where the price was low enough for buyers to overlook the sluggish performance – 70mph tops – and unsophisticated, angular styling.

ZIS & ZIL

Sounding like two evil twins, the company was primarily a truck builder until Party bosses felt they deserved to drive in limousines. The task of producing them fell to Moscow's Zavod Imjeni Stalina (renamed Zavod Imjeni Likhacheva in 1958), the first off the line in 1933 being a Buick 90 copy called the L-1. For the next 65 years a succession of vast, chromed barges continued to echo the most offensive stylistic excesses of previous-generation Packards and Cadillacs, and while the technology employed was far from state-of-the-art, quality control was exemplary. Doubtless propelled by a fear of being sent to Siberia, underlings ensured that every car was run for exactly 2000 kilometres before being checked again and repainted ahead of delivery to the Kremlin or Lubianka.

LOONY LAWS AND DAFT DRIVERS

In Britain the simple gesture of flashing your lights at an oncoming motorist to warn him of a camera or speed trap constitutes a conspiracy to obstruct the police and carries a fine of up to a grand.

Short-sighted Spanish motorists are required to carry a spare pair of specs in their cars at all times.

In 1984 in Woodbridge, New Jersey, a law was passed making it illegal for motorists to drive while listening to music. In the same state it's also an offence to frown at a policeman even if he's giving you a ticket.

Motorists in Pleasantville, Iowa, are technically still required to drive behind 'a herald carrying a bright red lantern' if travelling through the town after dark.

Barmen in Quebec are not allowed to sell Indians anti-freeze, nor must motorists in Montreal shave while driving.

Since 1864 it's been permissible to park any vehicle anywhere on the streets of Milwaukee for up to two hours – providing it's hitched to a horse.

On Guernsey the famous dairy cows are forbidden to walk the wrong way up one-way streets.

The Swiss banned motor racing outright in the 1950s – the Swiss GP was briefly run in neighbouring France – but in Belgium it's only illegal to race ostriches on the highway.

In Florida elephants mustn't be tethered to a parking meter without paying the appropriate amount.

The distinctive shape of a London black cab has its origins in a pair of arcane regulations, namely a requirement to carry 'sufficient foodstuffs for the horse' – hence the hay bale-sized space next to the driver – and for the vehicle to have sufficient headroom to accommodate a gentleman in a top hat.

London cabbies can also refuse to carry you if they suspect you're a smallpox carrier or have the plague. Because they are forbidden to leave their vehicles by the side of the road, they can also ask a policeman to shield them with his cape while they answer nature's call against the rear wheel.

Cabbies in LA are similarly forbidden to wear skirts, on pain of a $600 fine, while their colleagues in Indiana can wear whatever they like as long as they don't tether a crocodile to a fire hydrant or allow an ape to smoke in a public place.

In California it's illegal to shoot any type of animal from a moving car – except a whale, apparently.

Italian women are technically forbidden to wash a car in the street, while in Kentucky a woman may not 'appear in a bathing suit on any highway . . . unless she is escorted by *at least* two officers of the law [author's italics] or is armed with a club.'

The Indian Rajah of Bwalpur once decreed that his subjects should look away as he drove by, but in Denmark members of the public are expected to bow to the queen's convoy as it passes.

Roadside motels in Tasmania are forbidden to serve food to passing motorists unless the establishment is equipped with a wheelchair and stretcher.

Texan state law allows dealers to sell cars on Saturday or Sunday – but not both.

According to a 1907 statute in Arkansas 'speed upon country roads will be limited to 10mph unless the motorist sees an officer who does not appear to have had a drink in 30 days in which case the driver will be permitted to make what speed he can.'

There's also the case of Mr George Floss of Banbury, fined £25 in 1975 for carrying a dangerous load after a PC spotted him taking an inflatable doll 'with breasts and other convincing attributes' out for a drive in the country. In his defence Mr Floss said his wife had just left him, and a bunch of mates had clubbed together to buy the doll to cheer him up.

Good job he wasn't driving through California. In 1972 LA Police Chief Edward Davis suggested a simple way of dealing with criminals. 'We have a moving courtroom on a bus and the gallows is towed behind it in a small trailer. As soon as the criminal is grabbed, we hold a quick trial, find him guilty and hang him.'

Chief Davis would clearly have had a field day in Kansas. During a 'Drive Sensibly' campaign in Coopersville, a Porsche driver called Rob Needham was clocked doing 157mph. Or in the Bronx for that matter, where 40-year-old Leroy Linen was banned from driving 633 times in less than four years. Or indeed much closer to home: in June 1969 police stopped an 85-year-old in a wheelchair being pushed the wrong way down the M4 by his 65-year-old son.

8

THE CAR IN CONTEMPORARY CULTURE

JONI'S BIG YELLOW TAXI: CARS IN SONG TITLES

2CV	Lloyd Cole & The Commotions
Buick 59	The Medallions
Cadillac Funeral	Peppermint Harris
Cadillac In Model A	Bob Wills and His Texas Playboys
Cortina	Fendt
From a Buick 6	Bob Dylan
GTO	Ronny & the Daytonas
Hey Little Cobra	The Rip Chords
Hot Rod Lincoln	Commander Cody & the Lost Planet Airman
Jaguar and Thunderbird	Chuck Berry
Little Deuce Coupe	Beach Boys
Little Honda	The Hondells
Little Red Corvette	Prince
Little Red Rodeo	Collin Raye
Mercedes-Benz	Janis Joplin
Mercury Blues	Alan Jackson
MGB GT	Richard Thomson
Mustang Sally	Wilson Pickett
Rocket Man	Elton John
Y-Reg (Austin Ambassador)	John Shutttleworth

RUNNING DOWN THE ROAD, TRYIN' TO LOOSEN MY LOAD: 12 SONGS ABOUT DRIVING (OR POSSIBLY SEX)

Cars & Girls	Prefab Sprout
Drive	The Cars
Drive My Car	The Beatles

Driving in My Car	Madness
Fast Car	Tracy Chapman
Greased Lightnin'	John Travolta
I Can't Drive 55	Sammy Hagar
Keep my Motor Running	Roy Orbison
Keep on Truckin'	Hot Tuna
Low Rider	War
Pink Cadillac	Bruce Springsteen
Red Barchetta	Rush

. . . although frankly for many of us there's still nothing out there to touch the Man in Black who 'left Kentucky back in '49/An' went to Detroit workin' on a 'sembly line.'

I'VE BEEN DRIVIN' ALL NIGHT: AUTOMOTIVE ALBUM ARTWORK

The Beach Boys	*Little Deuce Coupe*	32 Ford Hotrod
The Birthday Party	*Junk Yard*	Ed Roth Hotrod
The Carpenters	*Now and Then*	Ferrari 365 GTB/4
Chris Rea	*Auberge*	Caterham Super Seven
Donald Byrd	*A New Perspective*	Jaguar E-Type
Dr Feelgood	*Sneakin' Suspicion*	Rover P5B
Geno Washington	*Hipsters, Flipsters*	Opus HRF

The Guess Who	*So Long Bannatyne*	Chevrolet Bel Air
Jack Bruce	*Things We Like*	Ferrari 365 GTB/4
Jackson Browne	*Late for the Sky*	'54 Chevrolet
Neil Young	*On The Beach*	Half a Cadillac
Pat Metheny Group	*The Road to You*	Vespa 400
Russ Conway	*Time to Play*	Rolls-Royce Silver Cloud
Sparks	*Propaganda*	Humber Super Snipe
Spencer Davis Group	*Greatest Hits*	Mini Moke
Stargazers	*Watch This Space*	Austin Atlantic
ZZ Top	*Eliminator*	1933 Ford Hotrod

TOP 10 CHEVROLET CORVETTES

Besides being an important reminder that not all Chevrolets are rebadged Daewoos, no car exemplifies rock 'n' roll America better than the 'Vette. It's had its ups and downs over the last half-century, true enough, but it's also earned its spurs as an authentic automotive icon, the definitive US sports car. Surprisingly not all of them have been V8s, neither have all of them have sold well or deserved to do so. But the best of the rest are true blue-chip classics and, as well as earning a place in the marque's own national museum (close to the production line in Bowling Green, Kentucky), the 10 listed below remain more sought-after than ever.

1953 The Original
Although the material itself had debuted sixty years earlier in a dress designed by Edward Libbey for the King of Spain's daughter, the glass fibre-bodied Chevrolet Corvette was the world's first production car to be made of the stuff. Despite lacking the V8 'mill' which has since become the trademark of a pukka Corvette it's still a classic, representing a sincere attempt to build an authentically homespun sports car at a time when the American market was swamped by thousands of English MGs and Jaguars. As evidence of this, designer Harley Earl started out with a 102in wheelbase in homage to one of his favourites, Coventry's groundbreaking XK120.

1956 Corvette SS
The name came from a type of small, agile nineteenth-century fighting craft, with early press releases using the English spelling 'Courvette'. Once fitted with a more powerful V8 the creation of a competition version was inevitable, chief engineer Zora Arkus-Duntov clearly being inspired by the example of the Le Mans D-Types. His SS (for Super

Sports) used a much shorter chassis, lightweight magnesium construction and a fuel-injected 307hp version of the newly released small-block 4.7-litre. Juan Manuel Fangio was meant to drive it at Sebring but after he pulled out (concerned that the car wouldn't be ready) the SS was retired after just 23 laps.

1961 Corvette Ducktail

Corvette design has long been a process of steady evolution through small detail changes but occasionally more substantial steps are taken, such as Bill Mitchell's introduction of the so-called ducktail which not only looked better but increased its boot space by a full 20 per cent. It looked more European too and, together with a marked reduction in the amount of chrome, gave the car a much classier appearance and one which would itself evolve over the next twenty years or more without major change. It was always a car for Southern California, however, with the heater an optional extra and relatively expensive too at $102 over the base price of $3,934.

1963 Corvette Sting Ray

All Sting Rays are Corvettes but not all Corvettes are Sting Rays, the name being correctly applied to a golden era of Corvette production from 1963 to 1967. An instant hit – the factory was forced to bring in a second shift to meet demand when sales leapt by a staggering 50 per cent in a single year – both the traditional roadster and the new fastback coupe combined futuristic styling, agile handling and vastly improved performance. The split rear window was considered controversial at the time and was quickly dropped although today it is these earlier cars which collectors seek most.

1963 Corvette Grand Sport

A Sting Ray on steroids, the Grand Sport was brutal-looking, ferociously quick and clearly designed in a spirit of 'shock and awe' even though the phrase had yet to be coined. It was Arkus-Duntov's intention to dominate the US road-racing calendar – meaning the factory had to build at least 125 of the 6.25-litre monsters – but GM canned the project before the first five had even been fitted with engines. A number of enthusiasts finished the job off for them, but the expected results never came and the Anglo-US Cobras remained the dominant force for much of the 1960s.

1968 Corvette 427

Derived from the striking 1965 Mako Shark II concept, the 1968 car featured dramatic styling which successfully moved things on from the Sting Ray although the two had much in common under the skin. This model also introduced the practical T-Top, and a choice of 300 and 350hp small-block V8s for anyone who found the 435hp 7.0-litre too hot to handle. Fit and finish were never quite as good as they might have been, and some road tests criticised the car for its lack of handling finesse – but the car was cheap and great looking, and more than 40 years on, still is.

1971 Corvette 454

With stiff new emissions legislation, and safety guru Ralph Nader on the warpath, 1971 saw the last of the truly high performance Corvettes – for a while at least – with a 7.5-litre V8 giving the car a full 425hp before outputs began to tumble the following year. The styling suffered too – by 1973 the requirement for 'federal' 5mph bumpers meant the nose and rear end had to be redesigned – and by 1975 the big-block option was dead and buried. Leaving enthusiasts with an unappealing choice of just 165 or 205hp, it's little wonder that demand for the '71 remains strong among classic car collectors.

1978 Indy Pace Car

For a while, with additional pressure courtesy of the Arab oil embargo, show replaced go with offerings such as the limited edition 25th Silver Anniversary model and an Indy Pace Car replica. Featuring a garish black and silver paintjob, and a totally OTT silverised leather interior, owners also received a set of 'Pace Car' body decals although thankfully these were placed on the front seat and could be thrown away when you got home. Officially it cost $15,000, but many dealers were asking for $28k with some punters offering up to $75k, more than five times the price of a standard car.

1984 Corvette Clamshell

The sixth generation car looked all new and was engineered from the ground up to be America's quickest car with a 140mph top speed and a sub-7 second 0–60mph time. The vast clamshell body-moulding was slippery too, with a 0.34 drag coefficient (24 per cent better than before) and inside the car gained futuristic, digital instrumentation. *Car and Driver* magazine recorded its then-highest ever lateral acceleration, saying 0.90g 'practically trivializes the previous high-water marks . . . generated by such exotics as the Porsche 928 and assorted Ferraris.'

1990 Corvette ZR1

At the time a world first, the ZR1 came with two ignition keys, the first of these firing up the 350-cube, Lotus-tweaked V8 to unleash 300hp – 15 per cent more than the contemporary Porsche Carrera, despite using only three valves and one fuel injector per cylinder – with the second providing access to all 32 valves and 16 injectors so the full force of around 400 horses could be enjoyed. Chief designer Dave McLellan insisted it wasn't a gimmick but a wise precaution for any owner in the habit of lending his car to his wife or son.

LIGHTS, CAMERAS, ALFA!
GREAT MOVIES FOR MOTORHEADS

In 2009 the *Daily Telegraph*'s Erin Baker and Simon Arron risked the ire of a million petrolheads by listing what they considered to be the 20 greatest car movies of all time – and then leaving out *The Blues Brothers*.

1) *Bullitt*
2) *Chitty Chitty Bang Bang*
3) *Days of Thunder*
4) *Herbie Rides Again*
5) *Ronin*
6) *Le Mans*
7) *The Italian Job*
8) *Goldfinger*
9) *Two-Lane Blacktop*
10) *Vanishing Point*

007TH HEAVEN:
THE NAME'S MARTIN, ASTON MARTIN

In the original Ian Fleming novels 007 drives a supercharged 4.5-litre Bentley and, when that's written-off in an altercation with a baddie, our hero switches to a Mark II Continental with a 'Mark IV' engine. Despite the fact that the company never made such an engine, it went, 'like a bird and a bomb and Bond loved her more than all the women at present in his life, rolled, if that were feasible, together.'

Briefly, in *Goldfinger*, he's issued with a smaller DB2 Mk III from the Whitehall car pool – let's not forget that Bond's essentially a civil servant – and certainly by the time the world's most famous spy made it to the silver screen it was with Aston Martins that James Bond became most strongly associated.

The connection was accidental, however. The producers originally wanted an E-Type but Jaguar, not recognising the films' massive publicity value, refused to play ball leaving David Brown to reluctantly step into the breach with a series of Aston Martins. (Neither were Jaguar the only ones to miss the boat in this way: in the US, film distributors were so dismissive of 007's debut that they bypassed the major cinemas leaving *Dr No* to debut at an Oklahoma drive-in.)

Today though, everyone's aware of the value of this sort of product placement, and Audi, Ford, Renault and – ahem – AMC are just a few of the manufacturers to stand in line waiting to join Mr Bond in his adventures. As the following table shows, however, 007 and his cinematic masters have for the most part remained loyal to the same few manufacturers.

Aston Martin DB5	*Goldfinger*, 1964
	Thunderball, 1965
	GoldenEye, 1995
	Tomorrow Never Dies, 1997
Aston Martin DBS	*On Her Majesty's Secret Service*, 1969
	Diamonds Are Forever, 1971
Aston Martin V8 Volante	*The Living Daylights*, 1987
Aston Martin Vanquish	*Die Another Day*, 2002
Aston Martin DBS	*Casino Royale*, 2006
	Quantum of Solace, 2008
BMW Z3	*GoldenEye*, 1995
BMW 750iL	*Tomorrow Never Dies*, 1997
BMW Z8	*The World Is Not Enough*, 1999
Lotus Esprit	*The Spy Who Loved Me*, 1977
Lotus Esprit Turbo	*For Your Eyes Only*, 1981
Sunbeam Alpine	*Dr No*, 1962

FOR OUR EYES ONLY:
BOND CARS ON PUBLIC DISPLAY

Sadly Desmond Llewellyn – as 'Q', the Double-O Section's quartermaster, he was responsible for so many of the cars' imaginative modifications – died in 1999 after crashing his Renault Mégane. Many of the cars have survived, however, with those shown below currently on display at The Bond Museum in Keswick:

AMC Matador	*The Man With The Golden Gun*
Aston Martin DB5	*GoldenEye*
Aston Martin DBS	*On Her Majesty's Secret Service*
Aston Martin V8 Vantage	*The Living Daylights*
Aston Martin Vanquish	*Die Another Day*
Ford Mustang Mach 1	*Diamonds Are Forever*
Lotus Esprit S1	*The Spy Who Loved Me*
Lotus Esprit S1 Submarine	*The Spy Who Loved Me*
Lotus Esprit Turbo	*For Your Eyes Only*
Renault 11 (taxi)	*A View To A Kill*
Toyota 2000 GT	*You Only Live Twice*
Tuk Tuk (taxi)	*Octopussy*
Volga	*GoldenEye*

12 GREAT FICTIONAL SCREEN CARS

Batmobile	*Batman* (the George Barris original, of course)
Benny the Cab	*Who Framed Roger Rabbit?*
Black Beauty	*The Green Hornet*
Canyonero	*The Simpsons*
Chitty Chitty Bang Bang	*Chitty Chitty Bang Bang*
De Lorean DMC-12	*Back to the Future*
Deathmobile	*Animal House*
Ectomobile	*Ghostbusters*
FAB 1	*Thunderbirds*
Spectrum Pursuit Vehicle	*Captain Scarlet*
The Tumbler	*Batman The Dark Knight*
SLOW: the Super Luxurious Omnidirectional Whatchamajigger	
	The Cat in the Hat

AUTO CUE: THE CAR'S THE STAR

Even ignoring Bond and the obviously made-up ones – better still: don't ignore them, just keep reading – a number of cars, good, bad and ugly, have had a starring role on celluloid. Not infrequently they can be the best thing in the whole film, managing to capture the public's imagination even on those occasions (and I'm looking at you, Ferris Bueller) when the machine in question isn't even a real one.

1958 Plymouth Fury	*Christine*
1961 Ferrari 250 GT Spyder California SWB	*Ferris Bueller's Day Off*
1963 Volkswagen Beetle	*The Love Bug*
1967 Shelby Mustang GT 500	*Gone in 60 Seconds*
1968 Ford Mustang GT390	*Bullitt*
1968 Mini Cooper S Mk I	*The Italian Job*
1969 Dodge Charger	*The Dukes of Hazzard*
1970 Dodge Challenger R/T	*Vanishing Point*
1970 Dodge Charger	*The Fast and the Furious*
1971 Plymouth Valiant	*Duel*
1972 Ford Falcon	*Mad Max*
1972 Ford Gran Torino	*Gran Torino*
1976 Ford Torino	*Starsky & Hutch*
1977 Pontiac Firebird Trans Am	*Smokey and the Bandit*
1977 Chevrolet Camaro	*Transformers*
1980 Lamborghini Countach LP 400S	*The Cannonball Run*
1995 BMW 735i	*The Transporter*
2003 MINI Cooper	*The Italian Job*

WHERE ARE THEY NOW?

Just as celebrities tend to be date-stamped – apparently the actual date is on their backside, which is why they can't read it – famous cars have a finite lifespan too. After that the really famous ones – Bond's DB5, the original Batmobile – are quickly snapped up by collectors. When the rest eventually coast to a halt, however, they sometimes fare less well: a few find their way into themed exhibitions (Tennessee has a Cars of the Stars museum, like our own in the Lake District) but many former automotive A-listers simply fade away.

Miami Vice 'Daytona'
A pair of Corvette-based fake Spyders were used for filming the 1980s TV series until Ferrari's American importers objected and offered the producers the use of a genuine Testarossa instead. One of the Spyders seems to have vanished altogether, but the other surfaced at auction in early 2009 with the registration MI VICE and looking for all its fakery a good deal less dated than the series in which it once starred.

Morse Jaguar
Bought for £100 from a scrap yard, the late John Thaw's 2.4-litre Jaguar MkII frequently had to be pushed or towed into position before filming

could begin. Given away as a prize, and curiously enough won by an Oxford undergraduate, 248 RPA was later auctioned for £53,200 and is regularly seen out and about by fans of the marque and the programme.

McQueen's Mustang

For many the Holy Grail of star cars – second only to the DB5 – of the two cars used for filming the iconic chase in *Bullitt* one was so badly damaged during the scene that it was junked. But the other survived only to disappear into deepest Tennessee where it apparently still awaits the restorer's touch.

Lotus Submarine

It's said that when Bond switched his attentions from Newport Pagnell to Hethel, Lotus took three years' worth of orders overnight. By way of thanks the car itself was left behind when the film crew quit the Bahamas, eventually being rigged up with lights and turned into some kind of garden ornament by one of the locals. It has since been rescued by the Ian Fleming Foundation.

HERE COME THE GIRLS:
A MAN-THING NO LONGER

Lady Docker, the aforementioned wife of sometime Daimler boss Sir Bernard, was also the 1955 Women's World Marbles Champion.

Susanne Quandt, daughter of the secretive billionaire family which owns BMW, once changed her name and worked in the company canteen.

Rather than lose it to Mrs McQueen in a messy divorce, actor Steve McQueen donated his rare 1957 Jaguar XKSS – one of only 16 – to a museum in Reno, Nevada. Later he claimed it was only on loan and could he have it back. . . .

Charlotte Rampling once played opposite Graham Hill in a movie when the F1 World Champion scored a bit-part as a helicopter pilot in the low-budget 1974 thriller *Caravan to Vaccares*.

Lotus is so named because founder Colin Chapman used to call his wife 'my little lotus-blossom'.

Both Mercedes and the Lotus Elise are named after little girls. Mercedes was the daughter of motoring pioneer and Daimler board member Emil Jellinek, while the British car was named after the granddaughter of Romano Artioli, one of Chapman's successors as the head of Lotus.

In what now looks like a spectacularly patronising piece of marketing, the 1947 Volvo PV444 had dash-mounted flower vase in a bid to appeal to the lady of the house.

When it went on sale in 1974, blonde bombshell Britt Ekland was so keen to get the new Lamborghini Countach that she had one flown direct from the factory to America.

A Lyons court once fined a woman FFr2,500 for biting a gendarme who had booked her speeding boyfriend.

Flying round the world solo in November 1930, the racing driver the Hon. Mrs Victor Bruce switched off her engine over Hong Kong to observe two minutes' silence for Armistice Day.

In 1927 Miss Violet Cordery driving an Invicta 3.0-litre became the first woman to circumnavigate the globe by car.

From the 1931 Artena to the 1972 Fulvia, for more than 40 years Lancia cars took their names from ancient highways named after daughters of the rulers of Rome.

1940s racing driver Roberta Cowell was born Robert and flew Spitfires in the war before having Britain's first sex-change operation. Thereafter the first woman to qualify for the Indy 500 was Janet Guthrie in 1977, whose helmet and race suit are now on display in the Smithsonian Institution.

A former stripper turned racing driver, Hellé Nice (1900–84) could have been a French national heroine but instead she was ostracised by friends and family and died in poverty after racing luminary Louis Chiron accused her of being a Gestapo agent.

Since 1950 just five women have entered the grand prix arena with only two of them qualifying to compete. To date the 1976 British Grand Prix is the only F1 race in which multiple female drivers – Lombardi and Galica – were entered.

Name	Seasons	Entries	Starts	Points
Maria Teresa de Filippis	1958–9	5	3	0
Lella Lombardi	1974–6	17	12	0.5
Divina Galica	1976–8	3	0	–
Desiré Wilson	1979	1	0	–
Giovanna Amati	1992	3	0	–

Traditionally women drivers have fared better in rallying, with the 1962 Tulip Rally (incidentally the Mini's first international victory) seeing drivers Pat Moss and Ann Wisdom become the first women to win an international rally.

Over the next few years Moss scored three outright wins and took seven podium finishes to be crowned European Ladies' Rally Champion five times (1958, 1960, 1962, 1964 and 1965). Besides being the younger sister of Sir Stirling Moss she was married to another outstanding driver, Swedish rally ace Erik Carlsson.

She is, even so, eclipsed by Michèle Mouton, the first and so far only woman to win a round of the World Rally Championship. Following her victory in the 1981 Rallye Sanremo, Mouton finished a close second in the 1982 WRC – winning in Portugal, Brazil and the Acropolis, and failing to secure the top slot only as a result of her Audi Quattro's poor reliability. She was also the first woman to win the gruelling Pikes Peak International Hillclimb in the US.

One wonders what Dorothy Levitt would have made of it all. In her 1906 book *The Woman and the Car*, the pioneering lady automobilist advised her readers always to carry a hand-mirror in their tool kits. Besides its invaluable role in helping to restore a gal's complexion after a drive, she said, such a device can be held aloft from time to time in order to check behind while driving in heavy traffic.

9

WHEN NORMAL JUST ISN'T ENOUGH

A FOOL AND HIS MONEY: SUPERCAR WANNABES

If nothing else, at the strange end of the scale, cars like the Pagani Zonda, Tramontana R and Caparo T1 show that if you've got enough money and can buy-in the sort of guys who know what they're doing it's perfectly feasible to build a no-expense-spared, 200mph supercar. In happier times than now you might even sell a few of them, although so far no-one's come close to matching Ferrari, a company which – boom or bust – is alone in managing to design, build and sell an entire range of supercars, rather than just the odd built-to-order headliner.

Jaguar XJ220
When Jaguar first unveiled the prototype XJ220, claiming its quad cam 6.2-litre V12 would pump out 500hp, everyone said they'd never put it into production. In a sense they were right too, for when the car

eventually did roll off the line the sensational V12 was missing along with the promised all-wheel drive chassis. In its place was a noisy 3.5-litre six-pot borrowed from a Mini Metro rally car. It still had 542hp, and managed a memorable 217mph around the Nürburgring Circuit, but a price tag of around £400,000 (and a UK economy which had just driven off a cliff) saw more than a few punters offering to pay in order not to take delivery of the car on which they'd earlier paid a deposit.

Bugatti EB110

The EB110 suffered a similar fate, dreamt up by Lotus/Bugatti chairman Romano Artioli in happier times only to find that the number of free-spending millionaires was way down by the time the cars were ready for delivery. Technically it was an astounding machine with a 60-valve, quad-turbo V12 powering all four wheels through a six-speed gearbox and giving it a top speed of 209mph. It wasn't exactly a Bugatti though – most marque enthusiasts agree they stopped making those in 1939 – but 0–60mph in under 4.5 seconds sounded pretty good, even if Marcello Gandini's styling wasn't quite up to his earlier work on the Lancia Stratos. In the end they sold 126 before the company went belly-up and was absorbed into VW.

Cizeta Moroder V16-T

Produced by an unlikely sounding duo – automotive engineer Claudio Zampolli in a joint venture with the electronic music composer Giorgio Moroder – this 16-cylinder beast first appeared in 1988, the 'T' indicating the shape made by the transverse engine and longitudinally-located transmission. Built by a number of former Lamborghini employees it was the first – and indeed only – post-war 16-cylinder car and remained so until the appearance of the Bugatti Veyron in 2000. They sold a few – the Sultan of Brunei's reckoned to have a two, maybe even three – but today your best chance of seeing one is by playing 'Gran Turismo 4' on your Sony Playstation. Amiga's Super Cars 'Retron Parsec Turbo' looks to have been modelled on it as well.

MCA Centenaire

Built, as the name suggests, to mark the 100th anniversary of the Car Club of Monaco – MCA stands for Monte Carlo Automobile – the original plan was to build exactly 100 examples although the final total was substantially lower: one each in red, white and black, and a couple of blue examples to finish off. Around 455bhp came courtesy of a 5.2-litre Lamborghini Countach V12, but the project was later sold to a Russian manufacturing company which entered a so-called MIG Centenaire in the 1993 24 Heures du Mans but failed to qualify.

Yamaha OX99-11

With Yamaha active in Formula 1 in the late 1980s, the extraordinary OX99-11 was produced as a joint venture between the IAD design consultancy and Yamaha subsidiary Ypsilon Technology. Although the F1 team had little to celebrate, the road car project garnered plenty of publicity thanks to its outrageous design which combined tandem-seating, carbon-fibre chassis and a similar 3.5-litre 70-degree V12 engine to the racecar. Thus equipped it was slated to provide what at the time would have been the closest experience an ordinary (if well-heeled) consumer could have of driving a genuine F1 car. Unfortunately a financial crisis at home led Ypsilon's Japanese masters to pull the plug on the project, afraid that too few buyers would be found for the £800,000 device. Three prototypes were completed but no customer cars.

Monteverdi Hai

Before turning his talents to designing super-luxury 4x4s for the emerging Middle East market, Peter Monteverdi's most extraordinary creation was the low-slung Hai or 'Shark', an aggressive looking coupé which at SFr90,000 was considerably more expensive than either the Ferrari 365GTB/4 Daytona or Lamborghini's Miura. In the end it caused neither of its illustrious rivals any bother, as only four were built. It certainly looked the part but the Chrysler Hemi V8 was a crude device compared to the Italians' V12s, and probably the world wasn't yet ready for a Swiss supercar, even one capable of squeezing up to 450bhp and 183mph from its 7 litres.

Vector WX8

Another attempt by the Americans to take on Ferrari – Ford's GT40 being the first – the sinister black WX8 which appeared at the 2007 LA Auto Show was the latest chapter in a long-running tale of various Vector supercars which had been appearing from time to time since 1989. With a supercharged 10-litre V8 and a 'projected' 1,850bhp – thus dwarfing the output of Bugatti's vaunted Veyron – *Motor Trend* reported a top speed of 275mph although this has yet to be put to a truly independent test.

WHATEVER YOU WANT – WITH KNOBS ON

Once upon a time customising meant just that – the customer did whatever he wanted to his own car – but increasingly hot-rodding's come in from the cold, moving in-house with many manufacturers starting their own rodshops or, if there's one nearby that's for sale, bringing outsiders under their wing.

Abarth (Fiat)

Established as an independent entity in 1949 by Austrian Karl (or Carlo) Abarth, what began life as a team racing mostly modified Fiats gradually expanded to take in many different marques, categories and classes although today the brand is still most associated with diminutive Fiat 500-based pocket rockets. More recent efforts have been mixed, with low points including the Cinquecento Abarth and Fiat Stilo Abarth, although the smile-inducing brilliance of the current Abarth 500 means one is inclined to forgive them any previous mistakes.

AMG (Mercedes-Benz)

In 1967 Hans Werner Aufrecht and Erhard Melcher wanted to go racing, selecting a Mercedes as their base car because of its reputation for toughness and durability. Equipping an otherwise ordinary 300SEL saloon with a much-tweaked 6.8-litre V8 they won the 1971 Spa-Francorchamps 24-Hour race. Currently responsible for its parent company's quickest cars, most memorably the Mercedes-Benz CLK 63AMG Black Series, essentially a street-legal version of the 2007 F1 safety car.

M Division (BMW)

Initially intended as a racing-only department, the Germans only changed their minds when management difficulties in the Lamborghini-assisted Procar BMW M1 series required them to take the project back in-house. The first road-going project was the M1 since when enthusiasts have been able to enjoy an enviable selection of M3 coupés and saloons to play with as well as the slightly mad 200mph M5 Tourer and curiously ugly M Coupé.

John Cooper Works (MINI)

BMW's 'other' in house rod-shop, John Cooper Works is the result of Germany's 2007 acquisition of the famous Surrey-based Mini tuner. Range-topping 208bhp MINI Cooper JCW is the one to have, despite having buckets of torque-steer, but the convertible version – lacking stiffness, gaining weight – struck many die-hard Mini fans as a bit silly.

Quattro (Audi)

Named after the third-most charismatic rally star of all time – after the Stratos and all those Monte-winning Minis – this outfit has been responsible for one of the most comprehensive and well-rounded high performance line-ups of all time, including as it does Audi's RS4, RS6, new TT RS and of course the R8. Porsche helped with the first one, the 1992 RS2, but these days Audi needs little or no advice from anyone.

Renaultsport (Renault)
Building on the success of the punchy little Clio Williams, Renaultsport's commitment to the cause is seen nowhere better than in the uncompromisingly tough Mégane R26.R. No rear seats or radio, perspex side windows instead of glass, and an expensive carbon-fibre bonnet save a stonking 19 stone of wasted weight.

SRT (Chrysler)
Denoting Street and Racing Technology, in recent years SRT's been responsible for a battery of Chrysler, Jeep and Dodge product from likes of the visually powerful 300 SRT8 and 600-horsepower Dodge Viper to the frankly bizarre Ram SRT10 – a Lambo-tweaked truck engine in a classic blue-collar pickup – and the ghastly Dodge Caliber SRT4.

STI (Subaru)
Established in the late 1980s, Subaru Technica International set out to break the world speed record for continuous driving over 100,000 kilometres – mission accomplished – and to win the 1995 World Rally Championship which it achieved at the hands of the late Colin McRae who took the title at the wheel of an Impreza. At the same time it took steps to transform the firm's range of so-so roadcars, most obviously with machines such as the power-pumping Impreza STi 330S.

Team RS (Ford)
From the 1970 Escort RS1600 through the scary RS200 to the blistering new Focus RS, Ford has time and again shown itself to be adept at adapting genuine motorsport technology to real-world situations. Fans complained when the new RS appeared without the four-wheel drive of the rally car, but then the complaints stopped the minute somebody actually took one out for a drive.

VXR (Vauxhall)
Developed from the VX Racing team's success in the British Touring Car Championship, VXR's proved to be a bit of mixed bag with wild highlights (such as the 237bhp Astra variant) somewhat offset by the likes of the 'hot shopping trolley' Meriva. What were they thinking?

X-Power (MG-Rover)
Created in 2001, and surprising everyone if only by the speed with which its new Qvale Mangusta-based, De Tomasa Bigua-derived X-Power MG

SV carbon coupé was unveiled, from the start the company looked a bit too good to be true – and so it proved to be. With an £80 grand-plus price tag keeping customers at bay, the company was soon overtaken by 'events, dear boy, events' and with just 64 cars built the MG-Rover dream quickly crumbled into dust.

WHEN FOUR WHEELS JUST WON'T DO

The crude, over-priced X-Power SV was a bit left-field, but at least it still had the right number of wheels with even Rover appreciating that while it sometimes pays to buck the trend, four wheels on your wagon generally seems to do the trick. In *A View to a Kill* (1985) Roger Moore tried a two-wheeled Renault 11 – the craze for 007 memorabilia meant even this half-car wreck later sold for £4,100 – and at other times carmakers have experimented with two-, three-, five-, six- and even eight-wheeled designs. Eventually most came round to the idea that four was probably the optimum number, but not before trying out some authentically wacky stuff.

1911 Reeves Octoauto
Having previously designed a bus with rear wheels nearly 6ft in diameter, Indiana-based Milton Reeves conceived the idea that what the world needed most was an eight-wheeler. More than 20ft long, his creation was unwieldy to say the least; also horrifyingly expensive at $3,200 when

a brand new Ford Model T could be had for less than a quarter of the price. Keen to economise he quickly ditched a pair of wheels to make the Sexto-Auto, but then whacked the price up again to around $5,000 as a consequence of which he was unable to sell a single one.

1913 Schilovski Gyrocar

From the frying pan to the fire, the next innovation was to try building a car with only two wheels, the brainchild of one Count Schilovski, a lawyer and distant member of the Russian royal family but clearly no engineer. He called on Birmingham's Wolseley Tool and Motorcar Company to build a weird, gyroscopically-stabilised machine, and despite being successful manufacturers of ordinary four-wheeled cars, lorries, double-decker buses and taxicabs, they apparently liked the idea enough to invite the crazy Russian in rather than showing him the door. In particular the count was convinced his new vehicle would be of great military value, with no-one at Wolseley noticing that the Tsarist army was technologically just about the least competent in the developed world. In the event the Gyrocar never got anywhere near a battle, which was just as well given its lack of brakes, modest 16 horsepower output (it weighed nearly 3 tons) and immense turning circle.

1919 Briggs & Stratton Flyer

The Flyer was a classic American buckboard (i.e. one notch up from a soapbox racer) with two seats positioned side-by-side on a stiff wooden platform and a large bicycle wheel mounted at each corner. Power came from a puny 2hp Type D Briggs & Stratton 'Motor Wheel' slung out the back, making the Flyer a genuine five-wheeler albeit with only one-wheel drive. Despite having no body whatsoever, and a brake on only the single, powered wheel, the Flyer cost a hefty $200 yet remained in production for nearly four years.

1929 Morris 6D

The 6D, a 70mph leviathan derived from a version of the firm's 6x4 army command car, was powered by a 4.2-litre straight-six and sported an immense limousine body, hydraulic brakes and six wire wheels. Of course it looked and was ridiculous, and with a chassis-only price of more than £850 – this at the height of the depression – it failed miserably.

1932 Morgan Sports Model

Morgan built three-wheelers for more than 40 years, the first one appearing in 1910, a rare van version going on sale in 1928, and then shortly afterwards perhaps the best of the lot: the J.A.P. engined Sports,

Super Sports and Super Sports Aero. The essentials remained the same for all three versions – independent front suspension, two wheels at the front, and one behind providing the power – but a tuned vee-twin engine and modified bodywork with two, one or no doors at all turned it into a proper little sports car. For many, even now, it remains the definitive Morgan.

1970 Bond Bug
Orange, unlovely but an authentic 1970s icon, the Bug was styled by Ogle's Tom Karen and was the first example of a new car design being modelled on a wedge of Red Leicester cheese. With a 700cc Reliant engine and a chassis from the same company's Regal, it was officially available in any colour you liked so long as it was tangerine although half a dozen white ones were later produced as part of a Rothmans cigarette promotion. With sales boosted by a successful Corgi toy it has a fanatical following today and is inexplicably much sought after.

1974 Tyrrell P34
The most successful F1 six-wheeler (in that Jody Scheckter managed to win a race driving one of them), Tyrrell sought to reduce the car's frontal area by using smaller wheels and compensating for the loss of contact area by doubling their number. Like Brabham's equally radical 'fan-car' the authorities promptly banned it but not before March, Williams and even Ferrari had chipped in with their own versions. These differed in that they had four wheels at the back to increase traction, but while tested extensively they too fell foul of the ban in F1 of four-wheel drive and none of the three ever made it to a race.

1977 Panther 6
Designed and built by Surrey-based Panther Westwinds, the 6 was an extravagantly styled convertible powered by a mid-mounted 8.2-litre Caddy V8 with twin turbochargers and a rumoured 600bhp. With advanced electronic dash, an automatic fire extinguisher, a built-in television and even an early version of a car phone, it was apparently inspired by Tyrrell's P34 or perhaps Lady Penelope's FAB 1 from *Thunderbirds*. With Panther insisting it was good for 200mph+ it would have been the world's fastest road car but this was never put to the test and total production struggled to hit two.

2004 Covini C6W
Again inspired by the P34, but somehow taking three decades to reach fruition, perhaps the strangest thing about the 4.2-litre Audi V8-powered C6W is its promotion as a safer alternative to more conventional car

designs. The theory goes that the six-wheel layout reduces the risk of a tyre blow-out, minimises the opportunity for aquaplaning, and allows for better absorption in the event of a head-on collision. That said, it's hard not to think that the risk of all three of these potential mishaps might just as well be reduced by not tooling around town at 185mph.

2004 KAZ Eliica
And finally, coming full circle, it's back to eight wheels. The KAZ bit of the name is actually Japanese, the car having been conceived, designed and built by a group of students at Tokyo's Keio University. And Eliica stands for Electric Lithium-Ion Car, although as the eight wheels suggest this one's not got that much in common with all those plastic G-Wiz things parking for nothing in central London. An authentic if unconventional supercar, the green-fuelled Eliica can accelerate from 0–60 in under 4 seconds and on a trip to Europe managed to hit 230mph at Italy's high speed Nardo circuit.

HOW LOW CAN YOU GO?
THE WORLD'S FLATTEST CARS

1966 Ford GT40
Primarily a racing car but they sold seven road going versions, including one to game-show host Noel Edmonds back in the days when he was a DJ. Famously named because it was so low – just 40in overall – the doors had to be cut into the roof so the racing drivers wouldn't brain themselves climbing in or Edmonds mess up his lovely hair.

1968 Lotus Europa Twin Cam
What Ford started, Lotus carried on with the Europa Twin Cam, for years the world's lowest car at a little over 3 feet. Aside from the usual Lotus niggles it was good too, at least once they'd ditched the original Renault 16 engine and stuck in the one the company used in the Ford-Lotus Cortina.

1970s Kitcars
By the mid-1970s dead low was the way to go but even its keenest adherents could see the downside. Your average Covent Garden contortionist's act was kids' stuff compared to the torturous moves you needed to fold yourself into cars such as the Piper, Nova and Probe. Unfortunately the view out was of the guy in front's exhaust too, plus

nobody else could see you down there which meant the risk of being flattened was high – unless, of course, you were lucky enough to slip under that truck bearing down on you and come out the other side.

1990 Impressed
A home-built car and, as the name suggests, the donor was a Hillman Imp. Looking for all the world like it had been crushed by having Skylab fall on it, the 26in high car was created by Perry Watkins – proud UK-based builder of the world's first ever street-legal, Mini-powered Dalek – and his mate Danny.

1998 Low Life
In 1998 Watkins resurfaced again, this time with a radically chopped, sectioned and strangely elongated Mini with a Rover V8 – see p. 133 – trick hydraulic suspension, and 250bhp. At 172in long, 54in wide and just 24in tall the car rocketed into the 2001 Guinness Book of World Records as the lowest fully street-legal car on earth.

2006 Flat Out
Years later another custom car builder came gunning for Watkins, Andy Saunders accepting the challenge to construct an even lower car, at just over 21in, breaking not just Watkins' record but also his own, much earlier one with the aptly named Mini Claustrophobia at 34.5in. Saunders, incidentally, is also the genius behind 'Vancake', the world's flattest VW camper at 39.5in.

2008 Flatmobile
Needless to say Watkins didn't take any of this lying down, and in 2008 produced this Batmobile-like contraption to shave another 2 inches of the record. It's fast too – thanks to a scary-sounding jet turbine in the back – and officially, for now, at 19in, the flattest car in the world. That makes it pretty tricky reaching up to take the ticket in the multi-storey, but then again he can always drive under the barrier without paying.

GETTING *SERIOUSLY* OFFROAD:
FIVE AMPHIBIANS …

Amphibious vehicles can be traced back to the 20-ton Orukter Amphibolos of 1792 and new ones continue to appear from time to time. The technology is simple enough, and notwithstanding the experience of Alberto Ascari – he lost the 1955 Monaco Grand Prix after dumping his Ferrari in the harbour – many cars will float. Trouble is, necessity being the mother of invention, it is still demand which drives the industry and when push comes to shove nobody really needs a car that swims, or a boat they can park outside Claridge's.

1942 Halfsafe

A modified wartime Ford GPA (General Purpose Amphibious), the good ship Halfsafe hit the headlines in 1950 when Australian Ben Carlin and his wife drove into the sea near Halifax, Nova Scotia, with a compass and enough food for 30 days. 31 days later they reached the Azores, restocked and headed for Africa and Europe, eventually returning to Nova Scotia in 1957. By then the Halfsafe had covered some 39,000 miles, and Elinore Carlin had filed for divorce.

1963 Land Rover Float

Based on a standard long wheelbase Series IIa, the machine was designed to be fully air portable and effectively marinised by fitting a long breather pipe, a non-return valve in the exhaust, and twin rubber flotation tubes filled with exhaust gas. Intended to carry ten soldiers, plus their kit, it was actually faster in reverse than going forward but was still too slow to be sniper-safe. Taking too long to make sea-ready should the need arise to take to the water, the project was 'ditched' and today just one survives intact, at the Imperial War Museum Duxford.

1967 Amphicar

Commercially the most successful amphibious car of all time, with 4,500 built over a five year period, the Amphicar looks not unlike a Triumph Herald – whose engine it shares – but was actually manufactured in Germany. Despite a high price and the obvious corrosion problems (the body was standard steel) the car's ability was proven time and again with at least three Channel crossings, one of which was in the teeth of a Force 6 storm.

2003 Gibbs Aquada

Built in Nuneaton – about as far from the coast as one can get – the Aquada looks like an overgrown Mazda MX-5 and is good for 100mph on land and a jet-assisted 30 knots once the wheels are retracted. According to creator Alan Gibbs, the concept was 'new in the way that helicopters were new or Harrier jump jets were new' – most amphibious vehicles, he says, run out of puff at about 5 knots – although so far at least it seems to have made less of an impact.

2008 Rinspeed sQuba

Taking a leaf out of Bond's book, 007 fan Frank Rinderknecht reportedly spent three decades 'trying to imagine how it might be possible to build a car that can fly under water' – before fitting a Lotus Elise with three lithium-ion electric motors and a couple of Seabob jet-drives to make his dream come true. Trumpeting the sQuba's emissions-free green credentials – even the Motorex lubricants it uses are biodegradable – the Rinspeed boss elicited a genuine 'Eau-la-la' response from the media although the concept has yet to enter full production.

…AND HALF A DOZEN AIRCARS

Herr Rinderknecht notwithstanding, most of us would be content to fly in the air, and various attempts have been made at producing a working aerocar over more than 70 years. Things reached something of a peak in the immediate post-war years – driven by a renewed sense of optimism perhaps, and a belief that 'the white heat of technology' could achieve the impossible – but the dream has so far proved elusive.

1937 Waterman Aerobile

Originally known as Waldo Waterman's Whatsit, this early attempt at building a 'Ford Model T for the air' produced a high-wing monoplane with detachable wings and a Studebaker engine. Five were built but like many hybrids it combined the shortcomings of both its parents, being too heavy to fly well and too large and unstable on the ground.

1939 Pitcairn Whirlwing

Designed by Juan de la Cierva, the PA-36 Whirlwing was a development of the Spaniard's autogyro concept, the theory being that it would require a shorter take-off than a conventional aircraft or flying car. Visit cartercopters.com to see a rare one in action, and you'll get some idea of how it managed to take off but then never quite took off – if that makes sense.

1946 Convair Car

Theodore Hull of the Consolidated Vultee Aircraft company produced a small, lightweight aluminium car with the facility to bolt on wings and an engine which his employers snapped up when orders for planes dried up following the defeat of Germany and Japan. Sales forecasts were massive – 160,000 units at $1,500 apiece – but then everything collapsed

when a pilot ran out of fuel, was forced to land on a farm track and sheared off both his wings.

1946 Fulton Airphibian

Part-car, part-'plane, the Airphibian was produced in the early 1950s by Continental Incorporated of Danbury, Connecticut. A curiously egg-like device with four tiny wheels and a two-seat cabin, unlike so many other attempts to make cars fly this one successfully passed through the prototype stage, was licensed by the American Federal aviation authorities and eventually went into production. Chitty-Chitty Bang-Bang was way cuter, however, and the Fulton struggled.

1947 Whitaker Zucker

Whether flying or driving, this one looked disturbingly beetle-like, the insect parallel reinforced by the way in which the twin 16-foot wings were designed to hinge back against the body once the vehicle took to the road.

2010 Urban Aeronautics X-Hawk

The X-Hawk operates much like a mini Chinook but without the massive exposed rotors which make helicopters dangerous for personal or urban use. Instead the rotors are contained in large ducts which make up most of the fore and aft sections of the car body, unfortunately compromising the fuel efficiency of the vehicle. With a price-tag of around $3 million it is scheduled to go on sale in 2010.

BECAUSE I CAN:
A NUMBER OF OTHER EQUALLY POINTLESS MOTORING ACHIEVEMENTS

The world record for driving a car up on two wheels belongs to Swede Göran Eliasson who managed 111mph in a Volvo 850.

Covering 38,000 miles in three and a half years, American Stan Mott is still the only person ever to have circumnavigated the globe by go-kart.

An American called Charles Glidden in 1906 drove his Napier 4,900 miles along the railway lines from Boston, Massachusetts, before becoming derailed just 50 miles from Mexico City.

In 1930 two Americans drove backwards all the way from New York to Los Angeles.

Driving his 11CV Citroën for 19 hours every day Frenchman François Lecot covered a quarter of a million miles between 23 July 1935 and 22 July 1936.

Having never before contested a rally, Jenny Cariou decided to tackle the 1997 Peking–Paris Race – in a Morris Minor.

Elizabeth Junek contested the 1927 Targa Florio in a Bugatti Type 35B after first walking the course at a rate of 12 miles a day.

Receiving her thirty-fifth speeding ticket, Gerta Streicher asked a German judge if she qualified for a reduction by paying for a further 10 anticipated offences in advance.

After ploughing up 5 miles of highway in South Carolina, drunken farmer Anton Barton was made to pay $235,000 to have the whole road resurfaced.

The first vehicle to successfully cross the Sahara was a 1922 Citroën.

In 1939 Mercedes was still listing wooden wheels as a factory-fit option.

At a motor show in the 1950s Bristol Cars boss Anthony Crook dressed up as a sheikh and attempted to buy every car on the rival Frazer-Nash stand.

In 1966 Jim Parkinson's single-cylinder Rytecraft Scootacar – adapted from a fairground ride and borrowed from his next door neighbour – became the smallest vehicle ever to have driven round the world.

For a race in 1902 Charles Jarrott repaired his car using bits of a bedside-table which he smuggled out of the hotel in his trousers.

From 1958 to 1967 the Citroën 2CV was available with four-wheel drive – and an engine at each end. .

Kent couple Chris and Sue Glazier spent their wedding night on the M25 aboard a luxury coach equipped with a honeymoon suite.

Who said it wooden go? American Jerry Nickel's mahogany-bodied car has twin 8.2-litre V8 engines and more than 800 horsepower.

Weightlifter Richard Kirby was arrested after trying to pick up a policeman on his stag night. (The policeman was still in his car.)

Oakland, California, boasts the world's first drive-in diner for dogs.

Trendy and triangular, the original Bond Bug was available in 'any colour you like so long as it's orange'.

Using parts from his Honda Accord, and pre-empting Ford's Focus television advertisement, musician Bill Milbrodt made more than a dozen musical instruments including the Doorimba and Exhaustophone.

Riding an amphibious Vespa in 1952 Georges Monneret became the first man to cross the English Channel on a scooter. Possibly the only one, in fact.

In the 1920s, after accidentally dropping six cars into the River Thames, Chrysler salvaged the remains and reassembled them for sale.

In 1955 an optimistic soul entered the gruelling Mille Miglia driving a Citroën 2CV – and finished in 271st place.

The longest race ever run was the 1947 Gran Premio del Norte run from Buenos Aires to Lima – and back again – making a total length of nearly 6,000 miles.

The most boring film ever made isn't Steve McQueen's *Le Mans* but Fernand Léger's *Le Ballet Mécanique* in which the stars were several Bugatti racing engines.

UK couple Jean and David Davidson lived for more than a quarter of a century in a roadside Travelodge.

In 1904 Louis Sinclair MP argued in court that it was his parliamentary privilege to drive the wrong way down Regent Street.

10

WHEN THE GOING GETS TOUGH

SHRINK TO FIT

It's all well and good aiming high when life is good but when things get tough even the most prestigious manufacturers have to cut their cloth to fit. Over the years some of the greatest names in the business have looked down-market in a bid to boost flagging sales, and occasionally – as America's once 'Big Three' will doubtless be relieved to hear – they've even got away with it.

AC Tricycle
Hard to imagine a world where you could get a car on the NHS, and when the differently-abled drove different cars to the rest of us – but such a place existed and it was called 1947. Back then such devices were called invalid carriages, were conceived by the Ministry of Pensions and built by AC for whom the 7.0-litre Cobra was still but a dream. With three wheels, a weedy BSA single-cylinder, room inside for one, and any colour you liked so long as it was bathroom-blue, production continued for almost three decades making this the most successful AC ever.

Alfa Romeo Alfasud
Built at a brand new factory down south in Naples (hence the 'Sud' bit) the baby Alfa was more bulbous than beautiful, its build-quality was typically 1970s – and, worse still, typically 1970s Italian – but it was a hit in 1972 and a sure-fire classic today.

Essentially the brainchild of one man (Rudolf Hruska, ex-Porsche) it sported a boxer engine where, in effect, the top was at the sides and the bottom in the middle. The result was a nippy, lively little thing with superb, well-balanced handling thanks to an excellent suspension set-up and the Sud's unusually wide track. To drive it was to love it, and more than three decades later the same is true. It took upmarket Alfa where they'd never been before, but the grin-factor was undeniable and for many the chuckable Sud is easily the equal of any pre-war Alfa supercar.

Aston Martin Atom

With more ups and downs than a Coney Island switchback, Aston's financial history has more than its fair share of red ink even though the cars have generally sold well enough. Unsurprisingly, the Second World War left the company high and dry, prompting it to resurrect a pre-war design for a lumpy saloon car with a modest 2.0-litre straight-four. Best described as ugly, the Atom's gawky shape thankfully never made it into production but is credited with rescuing the company when a drive in the prototype persuaded tractor magnate David Brown to step in and save the day.

Ferrari Ferrarina

Enzo Ferrari was famously disinterested in building road cars but still found the time to think up the tiny 'Ferrarina' – so-called, as it was never badged as such – and to his credit there was nothing half-baked about the proposal. Styled by Guigiaro at Bertone, with disc-brakes all round and a new Bizzarrini chassis impressively close to GTO spec, the car's sophisticated double-overhead camshaft 850cc four-pot was nothing less than two-thirds of one bank of a proper Ferrari V12 engine.

Ferrari himself used one as his daily driver for a year but then went off the idea which was mothballed until a group of rich enthusiasts decided to take it on. Renamed the Autocostruzioni Societa per Azioni (or ASA) Mille – with the badge somewhat curiously depicting a machine gun – the engine was expanded to 1,032cc and it remained in production until 1967. Too expensive and lacking the cachet of a genuine 'baby' Ferrari, it sold in only tiny numbers and when the project was wound up it's likely that fewer than 50 had actually been completed.

BMW Isetta

Things at BMW were far from good in 1945, with one factory trashed by the Allies and another suddenly finding itself on the wrong side of the Iron Curtain. Ten years on, sales were still dangerously slow so a decision was taken to move into the thriving microcar market by acquiring the rights to build a version of Italy's Isetta three-wheeler. The styling was tweaked a bit, the Italian engine replaced with a more reliable 245cc BMW motorcycle unit, and eventually the range was extended to include convertible, coupé and four-seat saloon versions. BMW bigwigs probably blush to think about it now, but altogether nearly 385,000 Beemer bubbles found new homes.

Rolls-Royce Legalimit

An early attempt to respond to changing times, when the traditional, horsey establishment kicked up a fuss about the noise and smoke from early motorists, Rolls-Royce's answer was a new V8 fitted with a governor to prevent owners driving at more than 20mph. Described as Henry Royce's one brief flirtation with folly – but then let's not forget he later considered ditching his famously iconic radiator grille too – this bit of nanny-statism thankfully flopped. Of the three built in 1905 only one sold (to newspaper baron, Lord Northcliffe) and thankfully none survives today.

Jaguar XK120 2.0
The XK120 was in its day not just the world's fastest production car – the name indicated its 120mph top speed – but one of the best set-up with steering, suspension and chassis dynamics every bit as good as its looks suggested. Exuding something of the most extravagantly styled coachbuilt Delahayes and Bugattis, being a Jaguar meant it was also dead cheap compared to anything which came even close to delivering this level of performance. Best of all was the engine, however, so how fortunate that the company killed off the proposed 'economy' version before it saw the light of day. The plan was to fit a mere 2.0 litres instead of the proper car's glorious 3.4 – one of the all-time-greats, designed in the dead of night by William Heynes and Wally Hassan as they fire-watched during the Coventry Blitz – but luckily it came to nought.

Panther Lima
Remembered now for monsters like the impossibly rakish J72, the De-Ville (as driven by Cruella) and the Cadillac-powered Six with its three axles and 8.2 litres, in the mid-1970s Panther attempted to create from the pig's ear of Vauxhall's parts bin something of a silk purse in the shape of the vaguely 1930s-style Lima.

Mercedes A-Class
Long before such phrases as 'credit crunch' or 'global warming' entered the language, Mercedes took the (for them) unprecedented step of producing a tall, short, one-box design with a modest 1.4-litre engine and none of the presence or patrician air we expect of anything with a tri-star on its nose. It was pricey too, and when one fell over after attempting Sweden's now-infamous 'elk test' many assumed the experiment had failed, that the car was doomed and M-B would go back to building what it knew best.

But no. Recalling the 2,600 cars it had already sold, and retro-fitting an electronic stability control system while modifying the suspension, Mercedes stuck to its guns, teased us with a very tempting twin-engined version at the 1999 Geneva *Salon* and has since gone on to sell more than 1.6 million of them. The success is richly deserved too, the A-Class being safe, clever – both the engine and gearbox sit beneath the floor – and well-built, even if it lacks the innovative approach and superior drivability of Audi's rival, aluminium-bodied A2.

10 BONKERS BUBBLE CAR DESIGNS

With the time surely right for a revival, micro- or bubble cars became hugely popular in Europe in the 1950s, a time when demand for cheap personal motorised transport collided with high petrol prices as a consequence of the Suez Crisis. Most of them were three-wheelers, which in many places qualified them as motorcycles (meaning low taxes and more lenient rules about who could drive them) and many of the best had their origins in Germany although one British bubblecar builder, Trojan, also built McLaren racing cars.

Messerschmitt KR175

Messerschmitt, for example, produced a series of cars which looked like a fighter aircraft cockpit because their wartime experience meant that was what they did best. Nor by any means were they all completely weedy, despite being based on an invalid carriage called the Fend Flitzer: a derivative known as the FMR Tg500, for example, is now highly collectible, the Tg denoting 'Tiger' and performance akin to that of an Austin Healey Sprite.

Maico Champion
Available in a number of different versions, including a now exceptionally rare Morris Traveller-style 'woodie', the Champion was designed to be built using only five body pressings thereby making it an even more viable proposition economically. Incredibly, and despite matching front and rear panels and doors which are interchangeable – tricks repeated by Bertone for a Peugeot concept car more than 30 years later – the 300cc Champion manages to look like a miniature 1950s Porsche.

Kleinschnittger F-125
One of the smallest, lightest microcars ever built, the open-top Kleinschnittger is said to have been designed to be dropped behind enemy lines by parachute – although the fact that it went into production five years after the war ended would seem to suggest otherwise. Capable of cruising at speeds of up to 43mph, thanks to a lightweight aluminium body and rubber-band suspension, the engine was later doubled from 125 to a heady 250cc by its scrap metal dealer builder Paul Kleinschnittger.

Heinkel 154 Kabine Cruiser
The definitive bubble car, with a front opening door, even bigger 'fishbowl' windows than the largely similar BMW Isetta and kiddie seats behind the driver, the Cruiser used a single-cylinder, 175cc engine created by Ernest Heinkel, the man behind the design of the first Saab road car engine.

Allard Clipper
Enjoying a reputation for scary, American V8-engined supercars, South London *garagiste* Sidney Allard celebrated his Monte Carlo win – his was the first English victory for twenty-one years – by launching the extraordinary one-wheel drive Clipper. It was the first car ever to have a plastic body, but unfortunately by placing the engine and chain-gear on the opposite side of the car to the driver in an attempt to balance out the weight distribution, Sidney succeeded in ensuring that every time one turned right the car lost all traction.

Frisky Sport
Neither frisky nor noticeably sporty, this optimistically-badged device used the same modest Villiers two-stroke engine as the Clipper, most of its energy being expended in producing sufficient noise to prevent any meaningful conversation between the driver and passenger.

Nobel 200
Built on the orders of 1950s carpet magnate Cyril Lord, the Nobel was based on the German Fuldamobil S7 and built under license in

Great Britain in the late 1960s. With a chassis fabricated at the Belfast shipyard of Harland & Wolff and a fibreglass body courtesy of the Bristol Aeroplane Company, the car's primitive specification meant it lacked a reverse gear. A quantity of unsold cars were later rumoured to have been buried beneath the A12 near Colchester.

Peel P50

The smallest car ever to have gone into production, the 49cc Peel took its name from the town on the Isle of Man and was once put on display in London's famous Foyle's bookstore mounted on a pile of books. With an overall length of 54 inches, and a single seat, it weighs around 130lbs and was originally sold for just £199 although survivors of the approximately 50 built are said (by their owners, this is) to be worth £25,000 at least.

Bamby

Similar commercial success eluded the Bamby, not least one suspects because at around £2,000 a second-hand Mini always made more sense. Today it is remembered not so much for the quality of its design and engineering but for enjoying the questionable distinction of being the only vehicle of its type ever to go on sale at Harrods.

Opperman Stirling

Arguably the rarest of all the bubbles, in that just one survives of the two which were built, the Stirling made its debut at the 1958 London Motor Show where it attracted considerable interest from both the public and the industry. It never made it into production, however, with many of the leading components suppliers refusing to get involved lest they upset Leonard Lord. As the boss of the British Motor Corporation he was about to launch the Mini expressly to get 'these bloody awful bubble cars off the streets.'

In the end, of course, the obnoxious and famously foul-mouthed lord got his way, and for more than half a century the Mini has gone from strength to strength. But these days surviving microcars have an avid following – see www.rumcars.org for more details – and rarities like the wonderful and wonderfully-named Goggomobil Transporter can still command high prices. The world's leading collector of such things is almost certainly American Bruce Wiener, who made his fortune selling bubblegum before opening the largest bubble car museum on the planet in Madison, Georgia.

TO THE VICTOR THE SPOILS:
10 EXTRAORDINARY MINIS

Broadspeed GT
As successful a Mini racer in his day as his more famous rival John Cooper, Ralph Broad sought to capitalise on the team's track successes by developing a steel and glass fibre 2+2 Mini fastback. Initially the plan was to create a series of luxurious conversions akin to the bespoke productions of Harold Radford and Wood & Pickett, but Broad's racing heritage quickly resurfaced and the cars soon took to the track with one of them memorably overhauling an AC Cobra at more than 140mph.

Mini Marcos
One of the more successful, long-lived Mini-based kits, the 1965 Marcos was a diminutive coupé with a glass fibre monocoque and standard Mini running gear. It was still in production 30 years later – restyled and now called the Midas 2+2 – but its finest hour came in 1966 when one of them was the only British car to finish the Le Mans 24 Hours although the car was sadly stolen shortly afterwards.

Minissima
A William Towns design using Mini subframes and an 850cc engine beneath a lightweight spaceframe construction and angular, aluminium body accessed via a single door eccentrically located at the rear. Originally called the Townscar, the interior contained two forward-facing seats at the front and two seats facing inwards behind, the fuel tank being located beneath the front passenger seat. Looking surprisingly modern for 1973, the only one ever built is now at the Heritage Motor Centre, Gaydon.

Ogle SX1000
Designer David Ogle's heavily restyled Mini dates from 1962, using a strengthened Mini floorpan and subframes with a new fibreglass coupé body. Dumpy and with slightly too long an overhang at the front, it was nevertheless comfortable and relatively luxurious although it struggled to survive the death of its creator (who crashed while driving one).

Quasar Unipower
I just love this car. Essentially a glass cube on wheels – and looking like it was constructed using several sets of Everest patio doors – the 1967 Quasar boasted unrivalled all-round visibility but lousy crashworthiness.

The brainchild of Vietnamese-born, Paris-based fashion designer N'Guyen Manh' Khan'h, and produced in tiny numbers in Perivale, West London, it was unique among car designs for its extraordinary transparent plastic seating and the fact that it was wider than it was long: 66in x 64in.

Radford Hatchback

A rare Radford conversion (see 'The Beatles and Their Minis', p. 99), an early car registered CPF 3H was equipped with a tailgate apparently at the behest of keen Mini enthusiast Peter Sellers. Sellers claimed he needed it to accommodate his portly fellow Goon, Harry Secombe, and it is thought to have cost around £2,600 or almost four times the price of a standard Mini Cooper.

Stimson Safari Six

Like an unholy cross between a Clubman pick-up and a gamekeeper's Argocat, Barry Stimson's strange six-wheeler sold in tiny numbers but at least one went for export and recently popped up in the Florida Keys with a price tag of $6,000. Closer to home another one failed to reach its reserve on eBay when the bidding ran out of puff at just £670.

Twini Moke

Co-starring with a Lotus Seven in TV's enigmatic/incomprehensible *The Prisoner,* and enjoying near-cult status as Britain's own beach buggy, the Mini-based jeepalike was conceived with the military in mind but the Army didn't like it. Two-wheel drive, tiny tyres and no ground clearance meant it was a lousy off-roader although, somewhat missing the point, the makers maintained it was nevertheless light enough to be carried over rough terrain by four squaddies. They tried to rectify matters with this 4WD Twini Moke – using two engines, one per axle, for better traction – before giving in and selling them to hippies.

Unipower GT

Designed by 'works' Mini racers Tim Powell and Andrew Hedges, the 1966 GT was an exceptionally low, plastic-bodied coupé using a mid-mounted Cooper or Cooper-S engine. It sold in reasonable numbers – around 75 – before the company responsible reverted to its normal business of building 4x4 trucks for loggers and firemen. A Mark II version slowly morphed into the deeply flawed AC ME3000, and the company was eventually absorbed into the BAE Systems Land & Armaments group.

Wildgoose Caravanette

A miniature camper-van based on a Mini van, the somewhat cramped 1963 Caravanette was built in Worthing and featured an extendable top, raised and lowered using a Heath-Robinson arrangement of a cable-winding winch and a bicycle wheel which revolved horizontally beneath the body. Bonkers.

Other titles published by The History Press

The Worst Cars Ever Sold
Giles Chapman
978-07509-4714-5
This book will take you back in time to when the family jalopy never failed to let you down, or that banger you bought from the local paper revealed its true character the moment you drove it – behold the worst cars ever sold and enjoy!

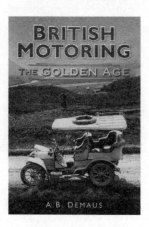

British Motoring
The Golden Age
A.B. Demaus
978-07524-5133-6
The photographs in A.B. Demaus's new volume date from as early as 1900 and recall a lost age in which intrepid motorists discovered the delights of the open road. At this time traffic calming, speed cameras and motorways would have been unimaginable.

Visit our website and discover thousands

of other History Press books.

www.thehistorypress.co.uk